UNFETTERED
FAITH

UNFETTERED FAITH

Bridging the Gap Between Science and Religion

SAM DELOACH

Primix Publishing
East Brunswick Office Evolution
1 Tower Center Boulevard, Ste 1510
East Brunswick, NJ 08816
www.primixpublishing.com
Phone: 1-800-538-5788

© 2025 Sam Deloach. All rights reserved.

No part of this book may be reproduced, stored in a retrieval system, or transmitted by any means without the written permission of the author.

Published by Primix Publishing: 08/08/2025

ISBN: 979-8-89194-522-7(sc)
ISBN: 979-8-89194-523-4(e)

Library of Congress Control Number: 2025912034

Any people depicted in stock imagery provided by iStock are models, and such images are being used for illustrative purposes only.

Certain stock imagery © iStock.

Because of the dynamic nature of the Internet, any web addresses or links contained in this book may have changed since publication and may no longer be valid. The views expressed in this work are solely those of the author and do not necessarily reflect the views of the publisher, and the publisher hereby disclaims any responsibility for them.

CONTENTS

Preface to the Rewrite...................................vii
Preface..ix

What is the Purpose of Reality?........................ 1
Thirteen-and-a-Half Billion Years or Seven Days: The
    Creation Story (Does It Matter?)...................... 4
What is the Cause of And Reason for Existence?......... 8
Can the Gap Between the Physical (What You Can Touch)
    and the Metaphysical (Spiritual) Be Bridged?........... 9
Pre-Genesis: The Time Before the Beginning 15
The Rebellion, Why?................................... 19
Existence, Why?....................................... 23
Standard-Bearer of Weights............................ 33
Enter Abraham... 40
What's Love Got to Do With It (DNA Swapping)?......... 44
This Ea Rthen Vessel.................................. 53
The Gift of Prophecy.................................. 65
The Essence of Power 79
To Talk A Good Talk or Walk A Good Walk 86
What's Love Got to Do With It?........................ 91
One Day at a Time..................................... 99
Who's Your Daddy?..................................... 107

A Question for You 116
To Do Good by Fighting Evil or to Fight Evil by Doing Good?. 123

Addendum to the Gift of Prophecy 128
Addendum: What Caused Adam and Eve to Fall from Grace. . 137

PREFACE TO THE REWRITE

I firs published Unfettered Faith in 2010. I wanted to know it was written in accordance with God's will, so I prayed He would see to its success, and to insure it wasn't selling due to my marketing it, I did't push it at all, which wasn't wise, for the old saying *if you build a better mouse trap, the world will beat a path to your door* rings true only if the world is aware there is a better mouse trap. There were also a few things that needed addressing, so in this rewrite, I intend to do just that.

It has taken me far longer to do this rewrite than I'd anticipated, for I felt unable to work long at all when I sat at my computer pounding the keys. I, at times, grew frustrated and wondered why I couldn't sit at the keyboard hours on end, as I was once able to do. I felt this way, despite the many physical signs I should have paid attention to.

A couple of years ago, I noticed that when sitting at the keyboard and resting my hand just above it, my right hand fingers would tap the keys involuntarily. I also felt extremely tired, a condition I'd suffered from for years, and my muscles, joints, and other parts of the muskloskeletal system began experiencing pain to a greater degree than I'd ever experienced or even imagined. I had been dealing with the latter for decades, but not to this extent.

A couple of years ago a Facebook group dealing with Agent Orange exposure on Guam convinced the EPA to test various sites we veterans who had been stationed on Guam in the seventies said were contaminated. They checked thirteen sites. Eleven showed evidence of Agent Orange being used on Guam. Forty years I had dealt with severe illnesses caused by this exposure at my on expense.

In January of 2024 I, after much persuasion, convinced the VA to let me see a neurologist to examine me, for I thought I may have a certain illness. They warned me against self diagnosis, but relented, and even allowed me to see a physician outside of the VA. In May I was diagnosed with Parkinson's disease. I'd been trying to tell them I thought I may have it for two years – two years I could have been taking much needed medication to slow the progression of this insidious disease.

Still, I have a purpose, and that is to tell the truth about the only known path to eternal salvation, therefore I write this preface after having edited and corrected the issues I felt needed addressing.

I may have and insidious illness, but I am saved, God is in command, and I shall soon enjoy a reality we cannot begin to wrap our minds around. Despite decades of suffering caused by Agent Orange exposure, I've lived a full life, have a wonderful family, and haven't had to worry about financial matters, for God has provided well. Why I've suffered the amount of pain I've endure for decades, I do not understand, but such has humbled me. When I get to heaven, I am sure I will be amazed at why God allowed this to happen, and I shall be thrilled by the answer.

In this rewrite, I am adding a few things I learned by doing research concerning more than one issue. Some of the time I spent in a wheelchair (I am out of it at the time) gave me more than ample time to think of many things where scripture is concerned. I think you shall find what I put for near the ene of the book very interesting. One issue I researched in depth has to do with original sin's cause, as well as what actual act did Adam and Eve commit that estranged them from God. Now, on to the book.

PREFACE

This work is quite unique in the manner in which it was penned. If some of the wording in this book seems strange (I speak of what I will do "tomorrow" or refer back to "yesterday" more than once), please understand it was written as a series of daily blogs. I never intended it to become a book, but once the words were written down, I knew what I needed to do, so here it is. It took just over three weeks for this work to be completed in the blogs I was posting.

As I began this series of MySpace blogs, I did so with great trepidation, for a couple of the subjects dealt with in these blogs are contrary to what I once held to be true. They are also converse to what many Christians hold to be true.

But there was a time when all Christendom believed, based on their interpretation of scripture, our solar system (indeed, the entire universe) was Earth-centric. Early postulates of a heliocentric solar system, including Galileo, were severely persecuted, and some were even put to death for their assertions. Time, however, has proven the heliocentrists to be correct, although scripture has not changed.

As I began writing this series of blogs, I did so with much prayer, for the last thing I want laid on my doorstep is the charge of starting and spreading apostasy. I dearly love God and would never want to do anything against his will. I even resisted the unction driving me to write this, but the compelling of my doing so would not silence itself.

At the time I wrote these blogs, I was living in Amsterdam, the Netherlands. I lived there just short of one year, although my wife, our fifteen-year-old son, and I were supposed to be there for three years due to a work contract my wife had signed with the company she had worked with for some thirteen years.

Near our apartment in Amsterdam, there was this beautiful park I used to visit quite often. Amsterdam was unlike any place I'd ever lived, for it was jam-packed with busy people. For a boy having been raised on a large farm in South Georgia, the hustle and bustle of Amsterdam was, at times, a bit overwhelming, and I found solace and respite in the beauty and quietness of the park. I would often go there in the early morning and feed the ducks, pigeons, geese, and sundry other birds eager for a meal free of toil.

I also became familiar with the various vagrants who used to hang out in the park and became friends with some of them. I found them to be very friendly, more so than many of the regular people of Amsterdam.

One day, as I sat on one of the park benches, I was praying earnestly to God to please let me know if writing this blog was indeed his will. It is hard for me to convey how greatly touching this subject troubled me, for I did not want to displease God, and I know many within the Christian Church will turn their back on me, including most of my relatives.

As I prayed fervently to God to tell me if this was his will (this was exactly what I was praying as this happened), a man whom I had never before seen in the park rose from the bench he was sitting on. He walked over to me and said in broken English, "I need to talk to you." He then walked back to the bench he had been sitting on and sat down.

I walked over to the bench he was sitting on (a bit puzzled) and sat beside him. As I sat beside him, I was a bit wary.

What really surprised me was he, besides speaking broken English, spoke Hebrew. He began by saying, "Mazel tov."

Mazel tov is a word I'd heard before, but I never cared enough about the word to actually look the meaning up until after he said it to me. I was surprised to learn it means "good luck has occurred" or "your fortune has been good" and is an acknowledgement of this. The phrase "Mazel tov!" parallels the use of the phrase "Congratulations!" and conveys roughly that "I am pleased this good thing has happened to you!"

He then continued by introducing himself. "I am called Shalom," he told me.

At the time, I thought *shalom* only meant peace, but I have since discovered it means much more. After a bit of research on the Internet, I found this written concerning the word *shalom*:

Hebrew Shalom . . . A word study in the New King James version for SHALOM says: Completeness, wholeness, health, peace, welfare, safety, soundness, tranquility, prosperity, perfectness, fullness, rest, harmony, the absence of agitation or discord. (Strong's Concordance 7965)

He then continued by saying, "I do not speak very often with people, but I have something to tell you."

His cryptic manner of speaking drew my attention immediately. For one of the few times I can remember, I just shut up and listened as he said, "You are standing before a mirror, looking into it."

Thinking back, this makes perfect sense, for at that moment, I was trying to understand my purpose in God's plan and wondering if it concerned the subject matter of the blog I was about to begin to write in earnest.

"You stand before the world, and you have a message," he continued. "The whole world is looking to you and waiting for you to deliver it."

My mind was boggled as he seemed to address the very prayer I had been praying moments before. I remember wondering how he could have known. He then said, "Do not look back."

No longer able to contain myself, I interjected, "You mean like Lott's wife did when being led out of—" I was going to say out of Sodom and Gomorrah, but he didn't let me finish my thought.

"Shhh!" he said. "Do not look back and do not look where you are. Look ahead, only look ahead."

The conversation then seemed to be over, and my senses were reeling as I considered what he had just said. I stood up as he looked out across the small grassy field in the center of the park. After saying a very short good-bye, I walked home, thinking about what he had said with great wonder.

I then felt strongly that God did want me to breach the subject I had so feared touching. Later that day, when my wife came home from her job, I told her of what had happened in the park.

She told me she thought the man talking to me was perhaps an angel sent by God to assure me that I, in writing on this subject, was doing none other than his will. This was the first time in over twenty years of marriage she's ever said such.

I laughingly replied since all the vagrants there were regulars, and he might be one who had merely been absent for a while, that if he were an angel, I'd never see him again. I personally had a hard time believing he was an angel.

The strange thing is, though, I never saw him again, although I looked for him each and every time I went to the park.

I resumed writing the series of blogs contained in this book shortly thereafter (I had posted one or two blogs prior to this). Within just over three weeks, I had all but completed what is now this book (all but the last few pages).

As I wrote and posted the blogs, I felt this (writing these blogs) was my sole purpose for coming to Amsterdam, for I do not believe I'd have had the courage to do so in America, where I would have been surrounded by those who would be adverse to its contents. I probably would have discussed this subject with them, and they would have discouraged me from doing so.

As I neared the completion of this series of blogs, I felt I would soon be moving home, although my wife still had over two years remaining on her contract as controller of European operations and no offers of a job or jobs from any other company. I even told a woman who read my blogs I felt we would be moving back to

America within three months, for my reason for being in Amsterdam had now been realized. You can go to my June 18 MySpace blog to confirm what I am saying is true.

Suddenly, something happened in her company she couldn't stomach, and when she came to New Orleans to discuss it with her boss (a new hire), he wouldn't even give her the time needed to voice her concerns.

When she was in New Orleans, she, given the opportunity, went to speak to another company about a job opportunity. There were others applying for the job; and when she left, she, like them, was told a decision would be made soon, and they would let her know in about a week. She was called the next day and told she had the job. Within three weeks, I was in my home in New Orleans.

I had also told the girl that if we moved back, we would not have to worry (much of my blog concerned this very subject), for God always takes care of those doing his will.

One thing we were concerned about was an outstanding 401(k) debt of close to ten thousand dollars. It was money borrowed to help us build our post-Katrina home, for the pre-Katrina was destroyed in the hurricane. If she changed jobs, we would be responsible for paying well over 30 percent in taxes, and as you know, the government isn't very understanding when taxes are involved. To say I was absolutely not worried would be a lie, for I too need much growth as a Christian (who doesn't?). Still, voicing my confidence in God's providence is a step which God will honor, and I have seen evidence of his providence so often in the past.

Then, as usually happens, Satan began to point out potential obstacles to God's will being done. The second obstacle, after the 401(k) problem, concerned when she was supposed to leave. She was to begin employment with the new company on the second day of August. But she was advised that if she left before the eleventh of August, we would be liable for taxes on over fifty thousand dollars.

She then had to call her new employer and tell him of her dilemma. He understood and said she could work over the computer to begin setting up the accounting operations for the new plant, which would soon be opening near New Orleans, and it would not affect her pay as she would be paid for the full month of August.

On top of that, her old company, which had suddenly treated her so badly as to make her leave, agreed to pay her for a full month if she would help with the transition. And she would have to only work for eleven days to garner this extra salary. God is awesome indeed, for we had sold her car before going overseas, and this is a good down payment on a new one even after paying the 401(k) taxes. God doesn't miss a beat.

If you would like evidence of such in your life, it is entirely possible, for God wishes to do the same for all of us. Read what I have to say in this book; even though some might be hard to understand and even harder to accept. This I understand, for I too had a hard time grasping what is written herein.

WHAT IS THE PURPOSE OF REALITY?

Have you ever wondered why you are walking this plane of existence? Or have you considered how and why this material world in which we find ourselves came to be—you know, everything from the smallest particle to the entire universe, which seems to expand every time new technologies enable us to peer further into the starlit darkness of its seemingly infinite depths?

I remember first asking myself the title question of this chapter in the second grade as I was looking at a classmate named Bodie Sanders. Why the expression on his face that morning prompted me to wonder such, I'll never know, but I can still remember his face and recall my thought (why are we here?) as the moment unfolded. It has been a question I've grappled with now for over forty-five years—why *is* all that is, and what is my place in it (this grand scheme of things)?

I was the seven-year-old grandson of more than three generations of farmers living in a rural area in South Georgia. My father, now farming exclusively, worked road construction. He operated a road grader.

Where the above question arose, I'll never know, but it had been raised; and once it had, this question became a phantom I have shadowboxed for years, for every time I thought I had it licked, I'd get struck by some blow coming from a direction I had never imagined. Such is life where, in even the three major religions, doctrinal differences within each religion divide and separate like no cleaver ever could. Even the atheists and agnostics aren't in total agreement and ultimately believe (most do) there is no point or purpose to our state of being with all its trappings. I, however (perhaps it's my upbringing on a farm), see purpose in even mosquitoes, for their larva feeds small fish and amphibians, which, in turn, feed increasingly larger prey, thereby establishing the food chain.

I see order revealed throughout the universe, even in supposed calamity and disorder. When Katrina hit New Orleans and destroyed my home, it devastated a large, wide swath of land as it laid waste to both man-made structures and things of nature (from the shorelines to vegetation and animal life—all was affected). I watched in amazement as hundreds of trees in many different stands died shortly after landfall while others took four or, as of now, five years to die a slow death while struggling to live.

I was appalled as too many lush, green treetop canopies turned a dead pine needle brown before losing their cover as the ground became carpeted in the same dead reddish-brown color. Then I watched in amazement as tiny spears of slow small green missiles, shooting toward a sun they would never reach, broke through the carpet of brown pine needles. The roots of new shoots reached down with no competition where, before the storm, there was much rooted competition below and a sun-blotting canopy above.

Katrina had deposited a rich layer of silt over almost the entire ground surface and had enriched the soil greatly. My pecan tree—which, due to saltwater intrusion, barely produced pecans the year after Katrina—now bears bumper crops greater than I'd ever seen before the storm hit. I was amazed that in the midst of such devastation, there was a positive occurrence, and had the area been unpopulated, the storm would actually have been seen as beneficial in that it replenished the soil of much of the area.

Although many people's lives were devastated by the storm, I benefited from Katrina. Before she hit, I had a two-story home on the water. Now, in the same exact location, I have a three-story house with two wraparound porches, one being a balcony fourteen feet off the ground. I am not saying Katrina hit to serve my purposes, but it reinforced the notion that there is a purpose in all things, for before Katrina hit, I'd been flooded four times in three years due to my house being on a ground-level slab. Now, when I'm not in Amsterdam, I sit high and dry while rocking on my balcony. When you look around and see ever-increasing calamity and chaos in the world, just know the storm is coming and soon will make landfall. If that is the case, ask yourselves this: am I prepared?

To prepare yourself, do as I have done and am still doing: educate yourself. I was the first DeLoach in my line of the family to receive a college degree. I did so at the University of Georgia, where I earned a bachelor's in journalism. I then went on to earn a doctorate in a denomination I've since realized has doctrinal issues with which I do not agree (there is no denomination whose doctrine is perfect), so I no longer preach or perform any of the usual pastoral duties.

Still, I have much to say based on experience and education. If you are interested in taking a walk with me and exploring some issues central to faith and truth, I welcome you. As I said, there is no perfect set of doctrines in any denomination, for the apostle Paul wrote that here, in this realm, we do not see things clearly, but in the next, we will. So go ahead and disagree if you wish. My mind is open, for I have many times realized I was in error concerning certain doctrines I was sure of until shown differently, usually through some unpleasant experience (sometimes, we need a whop on the head to get our attention). My personal prayer is that I will always be open to true correction when needed. Since this has been my true and heartfelt prayer for a while, and I believe all true and fervent prayer is answered, follow me and see where this journey takes us. I plan on posting something every day as I explore the issue of existence.

Oh yes, and if you'd like, invite some friends—I like a crowd. Perhaps, by doing so, you will begin realizing *your* personal purpose.

THIRTEEN-AND-A-HALF BILLION YEARS OR SEVEN DAYS: THE CREATION STORY (DOES IT MATTER?)

When I was a youngster growing up on the farm, I used to go hunting at night. There were no city lights within almost thirty miles, and the view of the night sky was a thing to behold. I still remember walking an old gravel road with Grandma and her pointing up to a swath of stars strewn across the black night sky as they hang in soft, glowing milk-colored contrast. I remember her saying, "That is the Milky Way." At that age, I wondered if it actually had milk in it. I also thought there were tiny living cartoon characters and people inside the TV and radio.

The universe is an amazing place, and the further our technology advances, the more amazing and complex it seems to become. Once, we thought it consisted of a firmament that surrounded and moved around a flat Earth. We thought the Earth was the center of everything in the physical plane, even believing the sun revolved around us. Now those believing such were not stupid but merely ignorant. Stupidity is permanent, but ignorance can be overcome with education. With time and enough scientific evidence, Protestant proponents and even the Catholic Church's upper hierarchy (becoming educated) had to reverse their position to the contrary, which, I think, would have pleased Galileo and Copernicus greatly.

As our knowledge has increased, so have the boundaries of what we know to exist. We once thought our galaxy was the extent of the universe on one end of the spectrum (macrophysics covers this). Now we know there are billions of galaxies just like ours—and ours, by far, isn't even the largest—and our galaxy contains hundreds of billions of stars. On the other end of the spectrum (quantum physics covers this), we are finding increasingly small subatomic particles with weird properties that boggle the mind. In a sense, our world borders are increasing in two opposite directions as our understanding of our existence in the material realm grows larger and smaller at the same time.

Those once espousing an Earth-centered universe with a sun traveling around a flat disk were wrong on so many counts and voiced their beliefs vociferously. Copernicus wrote on *Revolution of Celestial Spheres*, which postulated a heliocentric solar system, but it wasn't published until after his death due to his fearing the Catholic Church. His book was placed on the *Index of Prohibited Books* by the church.

Galileo, with the aid of his telescopes, began discovering moons around other planets. He also supported Copernicus's view of heliocentricity. Under threat, he recanted his assertions. In time, evidence proved both to be correct. Still, it wasn't until 1992 that Pope John Paul II officially apologized and set the record straight. Were the supporters of an Earth-centric solar system and universe evil persons or liars because they held and championed an erroneous belief? Or were they stupid?

They were neither malicious nor stupid (the majority, anyway) but misinformed based on the information they'd been exposed to. Today, there are still many like these errant thinkers, but today, many scholars, educated agnostics, and such do portray those lacking understanding as being stupid or malicious rather than being misinformed or holding on to a set of beliefs they've always held dear and are having a hard time releasing. Many scholars and thinkers wrap themselves in the self-righteous mantel of intellectual superiority. This they do most wholeheartedly when discussing the age of the universe.

In our modern world those educated elites who would do this are analogous to the Catholic upper hierarchy of the early scientific age. They, from a position of superiority, castigate, chastise, and demean those believing in the creation story told in Genesis. When Galileo was espousing a sun-centered universe, the Catholic Church was extremely influential in the daily lives of individuals, organizations, governments, and even regions (some quite large).

The average person had little knowledge, and even less appreciation, for science than we can imagine, for we live in a world where science has unraveled so many deep mysteries during the past couple of centuries. The Catholic Church had power and used it to try and squash what they thought threatened their system of beliefs.

Those holding on to Earth-centricity weren't stupid. Many were quite the opposite; they had merely pursued and dedicated themselves to the study of the metaphysical and how it deals with the physical. Then and today, such people tend to wear the mask of moral superiority.

Those in the other camp dealt purely with the physical; perhaps because the metaphysical can't be observed in any quantifiable sense. Those in this group often tend to wear the cloak of intellectual superiority, as noted above.

Because we live in a physical world revealed to us by our five senses and because of science having proven itself reliable, today the paradigm has shifted, with science taking ascendency over religion in the minds of most people. Whereas scientific thinkers such as Galileo, Darwin, and such were once ridiculed and loathed by metaphysical thinkers and were portrayed as heretical apostates, the pendulum has now swung to the other apex of its arc. Many devout believers in a supreme being can't understand why supposed great thinkers can't just take the scripture for what it says—literally. In their minds, seven days will always be seven days.

Today, it is the religious crowd being ridiculed and loathed by those postulating science as the be-all and end-all. Many scientists wonder, with all the evidence to the contrary, how anyone with an iota of intelligence could possibly believe the earth was created in six days (he rested on the seventh). They point to the untold thousands of dinosaur fossils recorded and stored throughout the world and to the accuracy of potassium-argon or rubidium-strontium methods used to date objects many, many millions of years old—far older than the six thousand years many in the religious community believe the earth to be. Surely, they think, those believing in what they can't see are idiots to cling to such foolishness when they have an opportunity to see, feel, touch, and hold a fossil, which should conclusively convince them of the error of their ways.

The scientific camp holds the universe is some thirteen to fourteen billion years old, as leading scientists now believe. The other camp holds the universe was created in only six days. Many in both camps loathe and despise (something we humans do well) those in the other camp. There seems to be no way to reconcile the two camps without one side capitulating and crossing over to the other side—as if you can't be a scientific-minded believer in a higher power. To which I say rubbish. So you tell me, seven days or fourteen billion years? Think about it, and I will give you my opinion when I continue this discussion.

WHAT IS THE CAUSE OF AND REASON FOR EXISTENCE?

Yesterday, I began a series in my blog in which I plan to post a small piece daily dealing with the subject of existence (as in why do we or anything exist, and where did existence originate). I have a doctorate in theology from a small seminary and a bachelor's in journalism from the University of Georgia. In this series of posts, I will surely anger (without intent) Christians, non-Christians, atheists, Gnostics, and agnostics all, but when you hit the nail on the head, you step on toes (like the mixed metaphor?). If you even remotely believe humanity is on the threshold of something greater than our minds can begin to comprehend, I encourage you to read. If you believe, like I do, all things (including the universe) exist for a purpose, I admonish you to read. I know most of you do not really know me and may be thinking *Why should I read what this dude has to say?* Well, unless you at least give it a glance, you will never know. And maybe, just maybe, you will find a small arrow pointing you in the right direction.

CAN THE GAP BETWEEN THE PHYSICAL (WHAT YOU CAN TOUCH) AND THE METAPHYSICAL (SPIRITUAL) BE BRIDGED?

Our universe, as I have stated, is a wonderfully mysterious place with mysteries able to boggle the minds of the greatest thinkers ever to have drawn breath. It consists of four dimensions. Three are spatial (height, width, and depth) and one temporal (time). It also is made of energy and matter, both of which can be measured. Energy cannot be destroyed or created, only moved from one place to another in any of various forms. Energy can be formed into particles and matter (plants change the energy of sunlight into carbohydrates using carbon dioxide, an electron donor [water], and light energy [sunlight]). Now, as anyone having heard or the Atkins diet can tell you, carbohydrates definitely are matter that matters in that they are the primary food source for almost all life or the basic building block supporting carbon-based life-forms (carbon forms the backbone of biology [plant and animal] for all physical life on our planet).

Carbon dioxide + electron donor + light energy → carbohydrate + oxygen + oxidized electron donor.

Matter can also be changed back into energy when the particles are broken down. Fire changes matter into heat and light, which dissipates into that (air, water, etc.) surrounding it.

Perhaps the simplest definition of our physical universe is this: the universe comprises everything perceived to exist physically, the entirety of space and time, and all forms of matter and energy.

Most scientists believe the universe to be between thirteen and fourteen billion years old. Those holding there is no god once thought, as did most of the academia, the universe had always existed, but scientists now believe the universe to have an origin as stated above. Once, those holding there was no god used the argument that since the universe had always existed, there was no need for a creator.

When opinion shifted to most believing the universe did, indeed, have a finite point of origin, some scientists actually saw God's handiwork. In fact, the astrophysicist who found the evidence proving the universe is expanding (which led to the conclusion it has a beginning) actually said it was like "seeing the footprints of God." Still, those not believing in God held to their convictions by arguing that the universe and all its matter and energy came into being from nowhere and out of nothing. They can point to an origin for matter (energy), but what about the origin of energy itself? Until they do that, they can never disprove an originator (or God) of all that is, just as I can't prove by empirical evidence God does exist. So, what makes their position any more valid than the supposition of anyone believing in a supreme being? Don't get me wrong. They are free to believe as they wish, but to do so with such demeaning arrogance as many of them do is ludicrous at least.

Yet there are some in the scientific camp that actually believe there is more to this material world and life than what our five senses can comprehend or experience or that there is more than science is able to reveal.

In his book *The Intelligent Universe*, astronomer Fred Hoyle (Michael Joseph Limited [London, 1983], 11-12) writes, "Yet as biochemists discover more and more about the awesome complexity of life, it is apparent that the chances of its originating by accident are so minute that they can be completely ruled out. Life cannot have arisen by chance."

Professor Robert Jastrow (1925-2008) was a scientist with flawless credentials. He was the founder and former director of NASA's Goddard Institute for Space Studies, a professor of astronomy and geology at Columbia University (New York), a professor of earth sciences at Dartmouth College, and a recipient of the Arthur S. Flemming Award for outstanding service in the U.S. government.

He also had numerous other credentials and much to say concerning most preeminent scientists' antagonistic and even hostile views concerning religion and God's possible involvement in the creation of our universe and his ongoing participation in it. This he wrote about in his many books dealing with space exploration, science, and astronomy although he was an agnostic. I will list some of his writings below.

The astronomical proof of a Beginning places scientists in an awkward position, for they believe that every effect has a natural cause, and every event in the Universe can be explained by natural forces, working in accordance with physical law. Yet science can find no force in nature that might account for the beginning of the Universe; and it can find no evidence that the Universe even existed before that first moment. The British astronomer E.A. Milne wrote, "We can make no proposition about the state of affairs [in the beginning]; in the Divine act of creation God is unobserved and unwitnessed" (*The Enchanted Loom: Mind in the Universe* [1981], 17).

Now we see how the astronomical evidence leads to a biblical view of the origin of the world. The details differ, but the essential elements in the astronomical and biblical accounts of Genesis are the same: the chain of events leading to man commenced suddenly and sharply at a definite moment in time, in a flash of light and energy. Some scientists are unhappy with the idea that the world began this way (*God and the Astronomers* [1978], 14).

Theologians generally are delighted with the proof that the Universe had a beginning, but astronomers are curiously upset. Their reactions provide an interesting demonstration of the response of the scientific mind—supposedly a very objective mind—when evidence uncovered by science itself leads to a conflict with the articles of faith in our profession. It turns out that the scientist behaves the way the rest of us do when our beliefs are in conflict with the evidence. We become irritated, we pretend the conflict does not exist, or we paper it over with meaningless phrases ("ibid., 16").

Consider the enormity of the problem. Science has proven that the Universe exploded into being at a certain moment. It asks, What cause produced this effect? Who or what put the matter and energy into the Universe? Was the Universe created out of nothing, or was it gathered together out of pre-existing materials? And science cannot answer these questions. ("ibid., 113-114").

It is clear that even the most esteemed of academia have to admit science does not have all the answers, and it probably never will. A few honest scientists will admit this just as a few honest theologians will admit they too do not have all the answers, for no one does unless God actually does exist.

On the other side of the spectrum are theologians and pastors who have an education and surely realize the overwhelming evidence (geological evidence, fossil evidence, stars being far away enough their light would take billions of years to reach the Hubble, and on and on) proves the universe and our world to be much older than early man could have imagined (let alone have explained to him in the Genesis story).

The evidence is overwhelmingly clear—the earth and universe are much older than can be accounted for in Genesis. If you question this, I suggest you read *The Genesis Enigma* by a professor of physiology at Oxford University named Andrew Parker.

His book gives a clear powerful compelling argument as to why the Genesis account and evolution are not exclusive of one another. I found this book fascinating in that I had already realized that the order of creation in Genesis was similar to evolution, with the seas coming first, followed by single-cell sea organisms, then more complex multicell sea life, followed by land organisms, etc. and culminating in man (until now the apical creature, whether you believe in a godless evolution or oversimplified creationism).

I can understand an uneducated individual believing in the creation story and holding those believing otherwise to be apostates, for they are merely uneducated, therefore haven't the understanding to know otherwise. This is the reason for the Genesis account as given—the lack of understanding held by ancient man. Think about it, how could a god explain to ancient man the age of the universe? The average life span was less than forty years when Genesis was penned. I am sure the concept of billions of years was beyond the comprehension of any man of that time period, let alone the big bang, the evolution of the universe, and life here on earth.

How would man understand the incremental changes over billions of years leading to thousands upon thousands of life-forms here on earth (most now extinct) eons ago? Using literal interpretations of Genesis and not understanding metaphors, creationists argue that each day described in Genesis was a twenty-four-hour period. I understand this, for they are ignorant (lacking knowledge). But many Christian scholars preaching creationism understand the metaphor and say the word *week* in Daniel corresponds to years whereas in Revelation, many scholars think the three-and-one-half days is actually three-and-one-half years.

In 2 Peter 3:8, it says, "But, beloved, be not ignorant of this one thing, that one day is with the Lord as a thousand years, and a thousand years as one day."

Surely to argue seven days is seven twenty-four-hour periods in light of overwhelming evidence to the contrary is more than just disingenuous and, in some cases, done so to empower and enrich or at least maintain power. Or they may fear rejection, for I know I have. I should have written this long ago rather than sitting silently for years.

And what is any less awesome about a god who could merely speak all into existence as planned by him and then just sit back and watch it unfold as he tended to his project, thereby being responsible as evolution unfolded? And while all this was going on, do you think he had no plan?

Yes, I can't fathom all this coming into being from nothingness (which can't be created or destroyed since energy can't be destroyed and is already present), existing, and continuing for no reason.

What (staying true to Ocam's razor) is easier to imagine, billions of things coming into being from nothing or from one? You do the math, for today, scientists believe there are multiverses (multiple universes existing simultaneously). I will go with the belief in one originator always existing and believe he is the author and originator of everything and somehow exists outside of our time-space continuum, therefore isn't governed by it. Such is what makes him eternal, for time is a component of this universe but maybe not in all universes or realities.

If this is the case, he is eternal and would be a being beyond our wildest imagination. He would be the Originator, the energy source behind creation. This may answer the how-to existence, but it doesn't begin to answer the most important question—*why*. Being as you and I are central to this question, it is worth exploring and answering. Let's continue tomorrow.

PRE-GENESIS: THE TIME BEFORE THE BEGINNING

Have you ever wondered why, if God has existed forever, he doesn't go into any detail of existence prior to the words "in the beginning"? It seems if we knew a bit more about his existence and the existence of whatever reality was before Genesis, we could better understand our reason for being. But, for some reason, God saw no need to go into any detail of anything prior to the account of Genesis. Again, I ask you—why?

I like using metaphor, and here I will use a canine metaphor. Have you ever had a dog? I have, since I was a child, owned one almost continuously. Some were more intelligent, some more loyal, some more obedient, and some had a combination of these traits in varying degrees as well as a myriad of other traits shared by all dogs. Though some were what would be considered the "ideal dog," I can say I loved all but one (she loved to kill kittens, and I couldn't break her of this). But the most obedient yet fiery and spirited individuals were my favorite.

I love how dogs become part of the human pack and believe they are a member of the family. For people who have had more than one dog or both a dog and a child, you will know how a dog will also try to avoid being the least in the pecking order just like any other child or pup would do. I think, with their limited mental capability, they actually believe themselves to be one of us. That is, until they see another dog.

Anyone who has walked a dog knows what I am talking about. When two dogs meet, something magical happens, for any pretention of human nature suddenly disappears. I believe all things pine for the company of like beings—beings that, when they come face-to-face, evoke the feeling of mutual familiarity unavailable otherwise.

As much as I love my present dog, Chewy (the most intelligent and obedient I've owned), he, sometimes, is disobedient. Certain times, it's as if he is unable to control himself. He knows he isn't supposed to bark inside the house, but if another dog passes by the window, he (every now and then) loses it. Perhaps it is a female dog in heat or just his hormones (we humans love this excuse), but I cannot understand his actions any more than he can understand why his barking bothers me so. I mean, what if someone or something became upset when I tried to say hello to another human being? The truth is there is a gulf between any disparate beings that can only be bridged by complete familiarity.

Prior to Genesis, there was only one being anything like God. He, unlike any other being, was triune in nature—Father, Son, and Holy Spirit all wrapped up in one being. Even the angels were, and are, not triune, for they were only spirit and soul (mind). How then would he quell this void caused by loneliness due to his being one of a kind? The only way was to create a being in his own image, an eternal triune being he could incorporate into his own family. But he wanted more than just another being to keep him company. He wanted a complete family—a large family.

Enter humanity. When he breathed the breath of life (his Spirit) into us, we (before being dual-natured and consisting of body and soul or mind) became like him and were truly in his image. This Lucifer hated, for we then supplanted him in the pecking order of creation (there is a common theme in all things). After man's fall, we became like Satan, having only spirit and soul (or mind), but I digress, for we shall discuss this later.

God now uses the church (what does a bride do? Produce offspring) to gain the large family he so desires. A majority of those in the know believe there is little room left for membership in his family, and soon, the invitation to join will be withdrawn forever.

For those who scoff at the Genesis account (I believe it to be a metaphor for what I am explaining) and point to the big bang as the author of creation, I simply ask you to explain where the energy causing existence came from since, according to the law of conservation of energy, energy can neither be created nor destroyed but is and has always been constant. Some form of energy (I call him God) ushered all existing on this plane into being and is still at work creating a family, which is the purpose behind creation. We simply call it the universe.

Some prominent scientists and cosmologists now believe what they call a quantum fluctuation caused the big bang. They also believe, if this is the case, there exist multiverses (many universes concurrently in existence). If this sounds strange to you, remember Paul spoke of more than one heaven. There is also hell, thus we already know of three planes of existence: Earth, heaven, and hell.

This is why so much of scripture seems so cryptic to the reader and is so full of metaphor. God trying to explain to early modern man the true state of reality, with early man's limited understanding of science, would be akin to my explaining to my dog why his barking is unacceptable (the neighbors get upset). It is simply beyond my dog Chewy's grasp as to why things are as they are and bridging the gap between explanation and comprehension is impossible. I simply talk down to him in a manner I believe he comes close to understanding. Until science began to unravel some of the mysteries lately, we were little pups in understanding. Now we are able to (more so) become the knowledgeable children God wishes us to be. If you tag along, it will make sense if your mind is open, for only an open mind can be filled.

So what was before Genesis? One thing that existed was a lonely being pining for a family (though he had angels), which led to our reason for being and the invitation for all who would come to come now. The invitation is open, at least for a time. The day will come when, like all invitations, it will be withdrawn.

Tomorrow I will carry on.

THE REBELLION, WHY?

In yesterday's post, I wrote about a puppy's bonding with a family and how it sought to not be at the bottom of the pecking order in the family. Conversely, anyone who has owned a large (especially male) dog knows they must remain the alpha in the relationship between themselves and the dog. A dog's natural tendency, just like a child's, is to try authority. This is natural in both the dog and the child, but at least you can reason with a child on a level you never could with a dog. The dog wants to be the boss. It is their nature.

Disobedience—it is what began this messed-up state in which we now exist. People often ask why, if God exists, does he allow evil to occur. Had they understood scripture, they'd grasp the real reason evil exists.

Had they knowledge of scripture, they would understand Satan's rebellion is the reason for all the ills of society, not God, for disobedience is met with what? The answer is *punishment* (unless forgiveness is extended). So why did the need for punishment or forgiveness arise, since all, in the end will be either forgiven, or punished for eternity? What was this act of disobedience, and in whom did it arise?

First, we will talk about the nature of the being from whom the original act of disobedience sprang. He was the first creature created and the most beautiful of all spiritual beings other than the

Creator. Originals are hard to even duplicate, much less surpass. He also was the most powerful, wisest, and craftiest of creatures. When this being was created, he was given the name Lucifer (light-bearer). He held a special position in creation in that he was the epitome of creation. So what could have caused him to rebel against his Creator and, in doing so, lose his preeminent position and risk God's wrath (as well as one really, really big demotion in the order of things)?

Enter humanity. Imagine you've been the top dog (I am sure the angels believed themselves to be part of God's family), and suddenly, a family member shows up (or is born/created) who is much like the Alpha (made in his image), and you know the same isn't so for you. Adam, unlike the angels, actually had the Spirit of the almighty eternal God residing inside of him. This made Adam a part of God's newly forming family. It was a family of triune beings. Think there might be a bit of resentment arising in your heart if you were Lucifer? Keep in mind that scripture refers to angels as sons of God. In Hebrew they used the term bene he Elohim (sons of God).

Still Lucifer had known God in ways we couldn't imagine and should have known only goodness emanates from God. God's purpose wasn't to lessen Lucifer among ranks of angelic beings but to gain a true same-likeness family. Some angels were amazed and supported God's plan when it was made known. Some (Satan first, then those who followed him) didn't. One third followed Satan.

Even in our world, the boss has the last word. In the spiritual realm, God's Word is absolute. We in this realm may discuss the situation and its ramifications (Abraham did when pleading for Lot, and Moses did when God wanted to destroy the Israelites). When Lucifer found man was raised above him in that man, like God, was a triune being (three parts—body, mind, and spirit) unlike the angels (mind and spirit), he grew jealous and rebelled. Discussion was not considered. In case you are wondering where I garnered this bit of information, I feel I should explain. I came across the book of Bartholomew recently. There is a reason apocrcypha was rejected, and it is easy to see why this book was upon reading it. But the verses below do not contradict canonical scripture. I believe these few verses elucidate the fall from grace narrative found in Genesis, chapter three. You also have to understand the book of Bartholomew is filled with metaphor, as is much of scripture that's canonized. When David wrote in Psalms that he would mount up on eagle's wings, he wasn't being literal.

Bartholomew 4:25 flabbergasted me:

[25] And Beliar answered and said: If thou wilt know my name, at the first I was called Satanael, which is interpreted a messenger of God, but when I rejected the image of God my name was called Satanas, that is, an angel that keepeth hell [Tartarus].

This pretty much lines up with my assertions and definitely lines up with accepted, sanctioned scripture. Note, also, he refers of mankind (Adam and Eve) as being the image of God. It was that apparent – something we cannot begin to see, let alone understand. I cannot wait until God reveals what we now cannot see – our spirit endowed by God upon accepting Jesus as Lord and Savior. I imagine it shall be a thing to behold.

This event's occurrence is also mentioned in Bartholomew 4:52-55:

[52] But the devil said: Suffer me, and I will tell thee how I was cast down into this place and how the Lord did make man.

[53] I was going to and fro in the world, and God said unto Michael: Bring me a clod from the four corners of the earth, and water out of the four rivers of paradise. And when Michael brought them God formed Adam in the regions of the east, and shaped the clod which was shapeless, and stretched sinews and veins upon it and established it with Joints; and he worshipped him, himself for his own sake first, because he was the image of God, therefore he worshipped him.

[54] And when I came from the ends of the earth Michael said: Worship thou the image of God, which he hath made according to his likeness. But I said: I am fire of fire, I was the first angel formed, and shall worship clay and matter?

[55] And Michael saith to me: Worship, lest God be wroth with thee. But I said to him: God will not be wroth with me; but I will

set my throne over against his throne, and I will be as he is. Then was God wroth with me and cast me down, having commanded the windows of heaven to be opened.

Do not let the word *worship* alarm you here, for there is no good English translation for some of the Hebrew and Greek words used in the Old and New Testament (and apocryphal) writings. The term *latreia* and its cognates are directly associated with both service and sacrifice when directed toward God.

It might have been better if the translators had chosen the words *serve, service,* and *minister,* instead of *worship.* If this is the case, I believe God was asking Lucifer to assist man in becoming the child of God, or offspring, God desired. Satan wanted no part of this. Not only was Lucifer (now Satan) cast down, but he also led fellow angels (one third of the angels) to rebel against God and his plan to have a family of like beings.

An existence that had, before the rebellion, been perfect and sin-free was now corrupted due to envy and self-will—two traits that seem so human in nature but are actually shared by both animals and fallen angels, it seems. To make things clearer, we must remember what Jesus told Nicodemus in John 3:3: Jesus answered and said unto him, Verily, verily, I say unto thee, Except a man be born again, he cannot see the kingdom of God.

You see, Adam and Eve's original sin had caused them to die spiritually in that God's Holy Spirit vacated their bodies when they sinned. God cannot abide sin. Henceforth all of their offspring were born without God's Holy Spirit inhabiting their body. This applied to all of humanity like a blanket covering a bed. God's remedy is made on an individual basis when one accepts Christ's atoning sacrifice, and turns their life over to his guidance,

EXISTENCE, WHY?

Perhaps more is revealed about us in how we react to certain events (especially something terrible) than ordinary, everyday life happenings could ever reveal. Most thieves, hustlers, child and spouse abusers, drug users, you name it, were tutored into what they've become. Yet some, a very few, walk away (or run) from what usually entangles. When I was young, beginning at nine, a few things happened to me which greatly affected me as a child trying to understand the world.

I could have easily turned to the dark side, but I turned to God instead, and I believe he revealed himself to me every time I poured my heart out. I could have wallowed in guilt, but in God, I found forgiveness. If I am wrong, I will go to the grave happy, for only death reveals what lies afterward (for most people), and I am happy.

Both the big things (my marriage to a human angel, coming out of Katrina much better off than before the storm, being paid to go to college by having everything from books, meals, medical care, room and board, tuition, and all paid for, etc.) and the small things have affirmed my belief. I think it was my choice to believe in God without prompting that has enabled me to become what I am.

I now have a bachelor's in journalism, a doctorate in theology, and am an ordained pastor. But before going to college and graduating at the age of thirty-two, I was an uneducated (college wise) farm boy who was so unsure of himself and his place in the world. In other words, I was ignorant but not stupid. My college and so forth was paid for by Vocational Rehabilitation, a government program that helps those needing a new career. To qualify for Vocational Rehabilitation, I had to pass some tests.

The truth is, I had never considered myself college material, for educational importance isn't emphasized very often on the farm. To qualify, I had to pass some tests (one being an IQ test). My mind was blown when I learned I was actually in the upper 5 percent IQ-wise. At the late age of twenty-eight, I found an opportunity blossomed, caused by my almost dying three times within nine months due to diabetic ketoacidosis. I took full advantage and attended the University of Georgia. There, I first became intimately acquainted with the metaphor. Still, I didn't appreciate it fully until recently due to my writing poetry, science fiction, and doing much research on the Internet.

When I was young, I'd read scripture and took almost everything literally—a day was a day, Eve gave Adam an actual piece of fruit, the devil was a scaly snake, and so on. Even though I had a bachelor's degree, I bought into this during my studies at the seminary. But there I began to realize all isn't literal, for in the book of Daniel 2, Daniel interpreted a dream for King Nebuchadnezzar in which the king had dreamed he saw a giant made of various metals. The Coptic dream had to be explained by Daniel and had nothing to do with a real giant. God uses metaphor, for his ways are hard, even for modern man, to comprehend.

I know the next step I am asking you to take is a difficult one, and I know many will refuse to follow, but if you believe in a literal six-day creation period where the universe is concerned, I ask a few simple questions. Where do dinosaur fossils come from, and how can multiple types of very accurate scientific measures of age all be wrong? Knowing the speed of light, we can calculate the age of certain faraway stars in the view of the Hubble telescope and know them to be billions of light-years away. The sedimentary layers you see in the Grand Canyon (it's a mile deep in places) go back two billion years.

Explain the seashells near the top of some Himalayan mountains. So much began to point to the earth (much less the universe) being much, much older than a mere six to seven thousand years. To see all this conclusive evidence and ignore it would have been intellectually dishonest. But why would God (he cannot lie, or he wouldn't be God) give us the Genesis account?

The answer is quite simple as I touched on earlier. Early man could not begin to understand, for scripture (Isaiah 55:8) states plainly, "For my thoughts are not your thoughts, neither are your ways my ways, saith the LORD."

There are many things God simply couldn't explain to early man—some of the things being a round Earth, to lengthen a day, the sun wouldn't stand still, but the Earth would actually have to stop rotation (how he did this I can't understand, but he's God); why didn't Eve freak out when a snake began speaking to her; who were the people Cain feared since he was the firstborn and the earth was not yet populated; and so forth.

Since God couldn't possibly explain such complicated events to early man (knowing and understanding science seems to explain much in light of recent scientific revelations), God spoke in terms the people of the time could grasp by using metaphor. If we strip the metaphorical descriptions bare, science and scripture need not be at such odds (or odds at all).

Some of you are probably thinking if such is true, it diminishes the majesty of the Almighty. They think of one being able to create on such a grand scale in a short period of time as being beyond compare. But is a being who could speak his will into existence and then sit back and watch it unfold over countless billions of years until his desire is realized, no matter what unforeseen problems may arise, any less significant a being? And then to think he was having his servants (the angels) carry out his plan all along. How could he possibly explain this to early man?

Yesterday, I dropped a piece of scripture many of you had never seen before. In the eyes of many, it isn't accepted, but the same scripture was held sacred by many early Christians, and where it doesn't contradict accepted scripture, I do not dismiss is so quickly. The particular scripture I am speaking of is Bartholomew 4:52-53:

[52] But the devil said: Suffer me, and I will tell thee how I was cast down into this place and how the Lord did make man.

[53] I was going to and fro in the world, and God said unto Michael: Bring me a clod from the four corners of the earth, and water out of the four rivers of paradise. And when Michael brought them God formed Adam in the regions of the east, and shaped the clod which was shapeless, and stretched sinews and veins upon it and established it with Joints; and he worshipped him, himself for his own sake first, because he was the image of God, therefore he worshipped him.

Remember from yesterday, the word *worship* should actually be translated to the English equivalent of "serve" or "minister" to, and that he wasn't told to worship Adam and Eve, but rather he was to worship the Holy Spirit inhabiting them both. Small wonder he so hate someone getting "born again", as it reads in John 3:3:.

It appears the angels had an actual part in the developing of God's plan as it unfolded. Satan was busy. He was going to and fro. He was working. But, according to the book of Bartholomew, although he was the apex of God's creation, he wasn't chosen to assist God in Adam's creation. When you read of Adam's actual creation, it appears Michael brought together the necessary ingredients for the task, and God simply formed a whole grown man.

Why would it be described this way if it was to the contrary? Again, because such was too difficult to explain to early man. But today, we have electron microscopes able to delve into secrets early man couldn't have imagined (germs always existed, but scripture doesn't mention them, still they exist).

Germs also evolve, for a new flu shot is necessary every year as the old strains mutate and form defenses to old serums. It is a genetic mutation in the RNA of the flu virus, which enables the RNA-type viruses to mutate quickly. Smallpox and polio are DNA viruses and mutate at a much-slower rate, which allows a vaccine to be made to control them, whereas a vaccine for the flu virus needs to to be changed from year to year.

In more complex organisms, it is heritable changes (passed on to the next generation) that causes changes within a species. If the change aids the species in survival (survival of the fittest), over time, the species will become dominated by those having this change, while those not having such a change will (or may) die out. If the change is a detriment to the species, those having it will die out, and the change never takes root (white alligators and lions are such).

Some changes are neither advantageous nor disadvantageous, and in such cases, some in the population of the species may exhibit characteristics caused by the change while others may not.

Blue eyes are an example of such a change, for such occurred in Europe some six to ten thousand years ago. Brown eyes were once universal in humans. Now there are many colors of eyes in the human species, including amber, blue, brown, green, and hazel.

We have been able to map the genetic code of the human being with an accuracy that stands up in court. People have even been put to death, while others on death row have been freed due to DNA evidence. It is accurate to that degree.

It also proves all life on earth shares some of the same DNA, and we humans share some of the same DNA with what is called LUCA (last universal common ancestor).

If you wonder what the angels were doing prior to Adam and Eve's arrival, they were busy helping God create life in its many various forms. When scripture says God did something, that is both metaphorical and literal. In much the same way, God says he is responsible for Israel's destruction various times in the Old Testament, although foreign armies actually did the damage. God is using the angels in the same manner as if they are an instrument. A violin, although it creates the music, is never said to have written or performed a masterpiece, thus the violinist is credited when he plays his instrument.

The earth from the four corners of the Earth and the water

from the four rivers is pure metaphor in that we, all creatures, share the same DNA, which God caused to somehow arise from earth and water. He provided the necessary ingredients for these two substances the moment he spoke the big bang into existence, although it took billions of years to come to fruition as the pre-life universe evolved. The way our DNA is structured is what makes us all individuals. Humans share the same DNA, but it is sequenced differently in all individuals except identical twins.

Obviously, Lucifer was involved in this great endeavor, but for some reason, Michael was chosen to oversee the sequencing of Adam's DNA, and the result pleased God. Perhaps Michael, through countless generations, caused certain favorable individuals from the far reaches of the earth to migrate to the area where the Garden of Eden was located. The Middle East is the one place on Earth where the three races intersect and where there is the greatest chance of DNA variations meeting. Here, Michael was able to find just the right ingredients for God's purpose. But what may have so pleased God about Adam's DNA structural sequence?

There was a mutation (blue eyes are a mutation), enabling man to finally reach the stage that God's plan could reach fruition. Humanity had already evolved, for these were the men Cain feared in Genesis 4. But with the advent of Adam, man finally had the ability to reason sufficiently for God's purpose. Today, even modern man doesn't possess this ability until reaching the age of reason (age seven in the Catholic Church, varies for other denominations), so the difference isn't such a leap between pre-Adamic man and Adam. Since Adam could reason sufficiently, God was able to do as he had always planned—create another triune being, another being like him, for the first time in creation. This caused Lucifer to become Satan in that he rebelled against this plan.

Now that a man who could reason sufficiently was created, causing Lucifer's fall, God needed a duplicate so offspring could produce more like beings. How did God do this? He took a rib from Adam. But why a rib? This too is pure metaphor we couldn't understand until recent (relatively speaking) scientific and medical advances. A genetic mutation is rare, and it seems God wasn't defying the laws of nature in some willy-nilly manner to bring about his will, for if this were the case, there would be no evidence of dinosaur fossils, etc.

If, today, I really wanted to produce another human identical to one already existing, it isn't beyond the realm of possibility. Complex living multicelled creatures (remember Dolly the sheep in 1996?) have been cloned by lowly man. Wouldn't God have done the same in that it was probably much easier and would have conserved energy (not that God doesn't have plenty, but Jesus gathered the scraps of fish, telling me God isn't one to waste anything)? This makes perfect sense, since he is the one who dictated the law of the conservation of energy, and he, except when a miracle is needed, abides by his own laws. Eve's creation was just such a need.

Now we have Adam and Eve, so what does God need to do? To ensure a pure Adamic race with the ability to reason sufficiently, he had to sequester Adam and Eve. This he did by creating a garden named Eden. Knowing Adam and Eve had the ability to reason, God forbade only one thing in order to secure a pure, unadulterated line, for such a genetic leap could have easily been overwhelmed otherwise by Eve's breeding with pre-Adamic man. All other fruit (action) was good, but adultery was forbidden especially for Eve, for the race depended on her eggs (being in limited quantity, unlike if Adam spread his seed) not being "contaminated." I am not any way saying Eve had a desire for any human other than Adam.

Perhaps this is why, in the Old Testament, men (but not women) were allowed more than one wife. This would spread this genetic mutation more quickly across the planet. These men, being smarter, would be able to dominate pre-Adamic man and produce more children, thereby spreading quickly across the globe. This also would bring the rest of humanity into the fold where those born were capable of sufficient reasoning ability to be held culpable should they do wrong.

Satan, seeking to stop God's plan in its tracks, devised a

wickedly ingenious plan—seduction. This is described pretty well in Bartholomew 4:58-59:

[58] And I awaked my son Salpsan and took him to counsel how I might deceive the man on whose account I was cast out of the heavens.

[59] And thus did I contrive it. I took a vial in mine hand and scraped the sweat from off my breast and the hair of mine armpits, and washed myself I took fig leaves in my hands and wiped the sweat from my bosom and below mine arms and cast it down beside the streams of waters, in the springs of the waters whence the four rivers flow out, and Eve drank of it and desire came upon her: for if she had not drunk of that water I should not have been able to deceive her.

Some may find the following objectionable, but preachers other than myself have come to the same conclusion. It is hard to arrive at any other conclusion when reading even sanctioned scripture. Let me explain.

Eve was seduced and liked it (still a problem in many marriages), and it seems Adam went along and even participated in the forbidden. This is why Genesis says they were naked and knew of it. The sin involved their reproductive organs, and out of guilt, they covered their nakedness". Satan, although he used a man, claims doing so in much the same manner God claims he created Adam (although Michael assisted). Satan was the force behind the action. When I said she liked it, I wasn't speaking of the actual act, but of her belief of what she would become (based on what Satan promised) were she to eat of the Tree of the Knowledge of Good and Evil. This wasn't in my first edition, thus I am adding this at the end; after the original text ends.

Adam had been given what no creature, man, or even angel before him had ever been given— inhabitation by God's very Holy Spirit, one of the three in the triune God most Christians believe in. This made him like God in that he was triune (to think God would honor us so). He also gave him dominion over Earth. This, too, enraged Satan. He had been boss before. Knowing the truth,

Satan lied (the first recorded lie) and told Eve, contrary to what God had said, she wouldn't die if she sinned. He said she would be like the gods (with a lower case g). In essence, she switched allegiance, which enabled her to know good and evil, whereas she had only knew evil prior to this. This is a teaser concerning something I realized upon deep research into Genesis, chapter there. I shall delve deeper into it at the end of the book for continuity sake, amd out of a desire this read as closely as possible to the original publication.

Sin had the same effect on Adam and Eve it did on Satan—they died in the eyes of God in that they no longer had a place in God's family. They, like Satan, were cast out; Satan out of heaven, and Adam and Eve out of the garden. Paradise was lost in both cases.

Satan once again was lord of the earth, and all mankind fell under his auspices. Adam's original sin was now passed down to all generations until one came who had no earthly father and over whom this curse (original sin) held no sway. Death had no claim over Jesus, but I am getting ahead of myself. Just after their fall, Adam and Eve realized their existence, as well as all their descendants, had changed in a way they couldn't have imagined.

But God already had a plan to right every wrong. It was foretold when he cursed Satan in Genesis 3:15:

[15] And I will put enmity between thee and the woman, and between thy *seed* and her *seed*; it shall *bruise* thy head, and thou shalt *bruise* his heel.

Who were Satan's seed? Some believe them to be the offspring spoke of in Genesis, Chapter six, when the sons of God (bene ha Elohim) bred with the daughters of man (bene ha Adama). I hold them to be all who would never accept God (and later those who reject Jesus) are children of Satan.

For those of faiths never having been exposed to the reality of the one true God, and salvation through the cross, it is up to each individual to decide according to their conscience and actions based thereon. This, too, I have researched greatly after publishing UNFETTERED FAITH. I shall discuss this later, also, though I touch on it briefly in the next paragraph.

Not being as clear as I should have been in the first printing of UNFETTERED FAITH caused others to think I was saying there was a portal into heaven not involving Christ's death, burial, resurrection, as well as our believing in it's power to save one from the penalty of sin, which is death should they repent of their sin and ask Jesus into their heart. Getting saved is really simple if you believe what I just wrote, so what is keeping you from doing so if you are not 100% sure concerning your salvation? You had best be sure, for hell is real. In nineteen eight-five I spent four days in a coma, wherein I wasn't dead, nor was I unconscious – I was in hell.

Those who accept God's will and his plan as revealed to them (the New Testament plan is the gold standard and a must for those really exposed to it if they feel God calling them to repentance (and they mustn't reject the offer). Most Americans will have no excuse, I am sad to say. Through Jesus Christ, man's original state can begin even while in this body but will not be fully realized until the Rapture or death, whichever comes first. Thus is told in the New Testament. Peter describes our state in 1 Peter 1:23:

[23] Being born again, not of corruptible seed, but of incorruptible, by the word of God, which liveth and abideth for ever.

We believers are immature children of God, like little caterpillars unaware we will someday soar according to our true nature. But someday, we will take to the sky as creatures we can only begin to imagine. I've gone over a lot today and need to rest. Hope to see you tomorrow.

STANDARD-BEARER OF WEIGHTS

When I was in the seminary, I once delivered a sermon on a scriptural subject I'd never heard discussed before, nor had I heard the main quote I used to support it having ever been used, either. I remember the president of the seminary taking meticulous notes, for I believe he knew I was on to something. Ever hungry for the truth, I began to pray to know the truth, even if it disagreed with a particular doctrine being taught by this seminary (a dangerous prayer, for change usually only comes after upheaval). In time, I realized I could no longer preach in a denomination so readily dismissing new revelations as needed and offered by God.

I never caused the slightest ripple of dissension among the congregation (other than the fact someone who had been bringing many into the fold and into the particular church I was attending), for that is unscriptural. If you disagree with a certain doctrine, talk to the pastor (I did) and no one else. If what you believe is true, God will have true believers gravitate to whatever is closest to the truth (Paul said we now see dimly, but someday, we will know as we are known).

Did I not believe this, I wouldn't be writing, for I pray if it is false, God will show me, have mercy on me, and quash it without squashing me. I hope you pray the same even as you pray to know the truth when it diverges from what have been taught and believed to be true. Ecclesiastes 7:16 says "Be not righteous over much; neither make thyself over wise: why shouldest thou destroy thyself?"

A know-it-all, even if wrong, can be taught nothing. So what was the sermon I spoke of on?

The scripture I drew upon, and my leading argument to the point I was making, is found in Proverbs 16:11:

[11] A just balance and scales belong to the Lord; All the weights of the bag are His concern.

I believe all true sermons are God-inspired, and at first, I wasn't quite sure of the direction I was to take this verse. But as I researched the verse and made the necessary cross-references (I abhor scripture taken out of context), I became amazed at how many times scripture affirms God abhors false scales and those using them.

Leviticus, Deuteronomy, Proverbs, and Micah all have verses dealing directly with this subject (some more than once). I began wondering why no one seemed to preach on this, so I began to really dig deep. As I dug, scripture seemed to take on a life of its own. I mean, we all know God hates dishonesty, but why the emphasis on scales in particular?

If you think our legal system—with all its parsing, legalistic talk and holding judicial precedence in higher esteem than common sense—is diabolical, you will be glad to know the author of such twisted legalism was Satan himself. I can imagine Satan saying to God after falling from grace, "Well, this flesh creature wouldn't be so obedient if you allowed me to tempt him."

If you are wondering where I pulled that thought from (it is great to know the scripture), think of Job. This was exactly what Satan said to God before God allowed Job to prove that man could, indeed, be tempted sorely and still remain faithful. Satan is called the accuser for a reason. He, like a little child does when caught doing wrong, always points an accusing finger to someone else. This has happened throughout history as various faithful individuals proved

God's faith in his children was not in vain. Job, with unbridled faith, shut Satan up.

I can imagine Satan, after Adam fell, saying to God, "Well, your one shot failed, and they've proven themselves unworthy. In light of their failure, my disobedience doesn't seem so bad, does it? Forget your plan for a family of triune beings like yourself, and let's just go back to the good old days where I was, other than you, the number one being. None of them are faithful, so just give up."

As I say, Job shut that accusatory argument down completely. And Job emerged from the test better off than before. Case closed? Sadly, no, for Satan, like some maniacal lawyer, always tries another appeal.

Satan might try to be the prosecutor, but God (if you follow him) is the judge and defendant. Still, you have to admire one quality of Satan's, for he doesn't give up. That is understandable, for his eternal future also hinges on whether we humans answer God's call. The outcome has already been decided. It was foretold when God told the serpent (Satan) that Eve's seed (Christ) was going to crush his head. Satan, it would seem, should have known God's will is irrevocable and irresistible, but his metaphor has horns for a reason (would you want to headbutt a bull?). He doesn't give up.

Another argument of Satan's concerned God's desire to ensure the genetic mutation, allowing Adam's ability to reason, would spread across the globe. Satan desired to extinguish this genetic ability to reason sufficiently before it gained a strong-enough foothold from which it could then "infect" the rest of humanity with this reasoning ability. This is spoken of in Genesis 6:2:

[2] That the sons of God saw the daughters of men that they were fair; and they took them wives of all which they chose.

Almost every explanation I have ever heard or read (and there are numerous, Google it and see) says the sons of God were fallen angels who bred with women, and together, they gave birth to Nephilim. I always wondered how an angelic, spiritual being could breed with a flesh-and-blood human. The best answer to almost any question is usually the simplest (a hypothesis known as Occam's razor). Since angels cannot procreate, another answer must be found in order for the truth to be revealed.

The children of God are those who, through faith in God (both Old and New Testament saints) and those who believe in Jesus as Lord and Savior since the New Testament was proclaimed. I contend all descended from a pre-Adamic race of humans who originated before Adam, byt whose mental capability, or lack therof, precluded them for being judged guilty of sin.

Some not so random (angelically aided) genetic mutation(s) enabled Adam to have sufficient reasoning ability for God's purpose. This allowed God to breathe his spirit into Adam and Eve. Adam and Eve were to bear flesh and blood humans that he might garner the family he so desired, as through them a family of like, triune beings was to come. Again, they knew they were not supposed to pollute the bloodline. They, however, found the flesh of the non-Adamic bloodline appealing, and fleshly desire took precedence over God's instructions and what their ability to reason should have led them to do. Even then, the flesh worked against the spirit, which is why we are admonished to be led by the spirit and not the flesh.

Addendum: To clarify what I was saying, I feel the need to explain further. Throughout both the Old and New Testaments, angles appeared to various individuals' from Balaam (not that he was the first) to the Apostle John (Revelation), God has sent his angels to convey his will to humanity.

That a spiritual being can manifest as being fleshly shouldn't surprise anyone when you consider what Einstein had to say about it. According to his theory of relativity, energy and matter are interchangeable ($E=mc^2$). For those unfamiliar with what the symbols of this equation mean, E = energy, m = mass (matter), and c = the speed of light. In essence, they are one in the same in that matter is energy having mass and occupying space. We see this when a small quantity of refined uranium (mass) is converted into energy (largely kinetic and thermal energy). We re able to see the flash of energy, and hear the kenetic discharge in the form of a lorge boom. (addendum ends).

By the time Noah was born, the whole bloodline was corrupted except for Noah, his wife, three sons, their wives, and perhaps a few other people who decided not to enter the ark. This occurring bloodline corruption is described in Genesis 6:1-5:

[1] And it came to pass, when men began to multiply on the face of the earth, and daughters were born unto them,

[2] That the sons of God saw the daughters of men that they were fair; and they took them wives of all which they chose.

[3] And the LORD said, My spirit shall not always strive with man, for that he also is flesh: yet his days shall be an hundred and twenty years.

[4] There were giants in the earth in those days; and also after that, when the sons of God came in unto the daughters of men, and they bare children to them, the same became mighty men which were of old, men of renown.

[5] And GOD saw that the wickedness of man was great in the earth, and that every imagination of the thoughts of his heart was only evil continually.

Addendum: Genesis 6:8&9 reads: 8 But Noah found grace in the eyes of the Lord. 9 These are the generations of Noah: Noah was a just man and perfect in his generations, and Noah walked with God. Since Paul wrote "all have sionned and fall short of the glory of God", we know Noah wasn't perfect where sin is concerned. So, what did the author (ultimately God) mean when writing "perfect in his generations? He was speaking of Noah's bloodline (DNA) remaining true to what Adam and Eve had passed down; without adulteration, for, for God's promise found in Genesis stated that her seed (Jesus) would crush the serpent's (Satan's) head. This prophecy couldn't be fulfilled if no pure Adamic bloodline existed, and God would have been made a liar. That couldn't be. (end addendum).

I can imagine Satan going before God, saying, "Look how pitiful they are. Why don't you just give up? There are only a few left anyway. And of the few you have left; you know none will answer your call to safety should you decided to blot out this vermin you call man. You will have to destroy everything, including them, if you want to keep the bloodline pure. Yes, let's just turn the clock back [no clocks back then]."

Again, God, using a mere flesh-and-blood being, thwarted the designs of the most powerful angelic entity ever created. I know this has to stick in Satan's craw— God's ability to use the last in the line of fleshly creations to thwart the designs of the first and most powerful angelic being. It sheds new light on Matthew 20:16:

[16] So the last shall be first, and the first last: for many be called, but few chosen.

Noah, just as did Job, proved God's will to be perfect and irrefutable. So, Satan devised another argument in his attempt to thwart God's will and God's desire to create a family of like, triune beings.

Before I go into that, I wish to digress a bit. The Chinese language is pictographic, using a combination of simple characters to form more complicated words and concepts. Their character for *boat* combines the characters *eight*, *mouth*, and *vessel* to convey the concept of a flood. Why eight people and a boat? Noah, his wife, three sons, and three daughters-in-law add up to eight.

The word *flood* combines elements of the characters *eight* plus *united* plus earth, which equals the character *total*. When you combine the character *total* with the character *water*, you get *flood*.

Also, the Chinese written language developed shortly after the Tower of Babel took place. Much of the book of Genesis is hidden in the original Chinese written language. If you wish to further investigate this, read *The Discovery of Genesis: How the Truths of Genesis Were Found Hidden in the Chinese Language*. It is written by C. H. Kang and Ethel R. Nelson. The truth always supports itself even in metaphor.

The important point here is the descendants of Noah (the Adamic bloodline) did spread across the globe, for the story of Genesis is found in the Chinese characters. The Chinese written language can be traced back to around 2000 BC. Around 300 to 400 AD the Polynesians, who originated in the area of Taiwan just off the southeastern coast of China, spread across many of the South Pacific Islands even to Hawaii and the remote Easter Islands. It is very plausible, therefore, to conclude that the seed of Adam, even in a few thousand years, was able to "infect" all of humanity—even the Americas, Australia, and the far reaches of the globe.

Some might think a worldwide flood was and is impossible and say there is no geological proof. That doesn't matter. What does it matter if the flood was only regional, but it allowed the Adamic bloodline to gain enough of a foothold to ensure its survival? Or what does it matter if it was universal, and our simple mind can't wrap around the idea of such an event? To the people living in the area and recording the event, it would have seemed (or could have been) worldwide, and a metaphorical or literal description would have sufficed. Again, there is an answer to any question—some are merely wrong, and only one can be spot-on. You decide what logic dictates or what your heart tells you and then pray over it.

The next argument Satan used was his best attempt. I am sure—with his knowing how strongly we, as animals, follow certain instincts (one being the desire to procreate)—Satan was almost positive this argument would convince God he had made a mistake. I mean, who in their right mind would willingly sacrifice their only legitimate son?

ENTER ABRAHAM

The next argument Satan brought up was totally depraved and diabolical. After his fall from grace, not only was Satan no longer the ruler of this world upon Adam's arrival (this must have really angered him), but he had also lost his position as the chief archangel in the spiritual world. When he fell, he abdicated his position of authority wherein he was the boss out in the field, implementing the Chief Executive's wishes. His fall from grace infuriated the metaphorical cloven-hooved one enough to wish to destroy humanity – a goal he still harbors.

His fury was kicked up to the factor of infinity squared, though, when he learned the reason for, or cause of, his fall (Adam) was elevated to the lofty earthly position Lucifer had held before becoming Satan. So he devised the plan as I explained two or three posts earlier on this subject. Because Adam fell when he and Eve were deceived, Satan wrested control of earth back from Adam, and mankind fell under Satan's jurisdiction in much the same manner a servant answers to his lord. This is the reason even toddlers have a penchant for mischief. If you think I am being cynical, put two kids in a room, drop one lollipop in between them, and just watch. Afterward, teach them a lesson on sharing so the exercise will not have been a waste.

But the wonderful thing is, we still have the capacity to reason and, doing so, may realize our true state even though we are born as children of Satan. The seed, never accepting any shortcomings and who would bruise the heel of Eve's seed (Emmanuel) before Satan would have his own head crushed due to the crucifixion, is the seed of Satan.

Those accepting the plan of salvation are then able to live a life where a sense of justice is combined with mercy. In doing this, believers will be led to repent when doing wrong and do unto others as we would have them do unto us. A quick glance at the world today makes it obvious we haven't progressed very much as a race. Throughout history, only a few of any population have seemed able to grasp our need to reach higher than our eyes are able to see and we, like Satan, become tripped up by the flesh (Adam's creation got him). Again, what I find amazing is, using such a small percentage of the population, God has been able to frustrate Satan's grandest schemes.

Scripture reveals Abraham's birthplace as Ur of the Chaldeans in Genesis. One day, Abram (he doesn't become known as Abraham until later) hears a voice telling him to leave and travel to a place unknown. In our life, we, when we go from doubting God's existence to believing, do much the same thing—giving up the known for the unknown. Satan probably used this argument (why waste anything?) on God by saying something like "Just abandon them, they would never literally follow you into the unknown." Abraham was willing.

So Satan, because he had used our overwhelming desire to procreate in causing Eve to sin (while polluting the Adamic bloodline), decided to use this basic most powerful need once again. It seems Satan has fought time and again against God's will coming into fruition. This he did throughout Abraham's life (he does this with all of us). He realized Abraham was special, so he marshaled special forces in this battle.

This battle, because it took Sarah so long to give birth, took on special significance. In Genesis, Chapter sixteen we see even Sarah, doubt God's promise, admonished Abraham to do something, which proved Abraham too had his moments of weakness. Sarah, doubting

God's Word, had Abraham sire a son by his servant Hagar, who gave birth to Ishmael. The children of Ishmael are the ancestors of the nations surrounding modern-day Israel and who have promised to destroy her. Both sides are at fault somewhat in the Mideast. Disobedience sometimes has long-term implications. The thing is, both God and Satan saw something special in Abraham—perhaps his DNA?

Finally, well-past childbearing age (we can do that now with fetal implantation [scientifically feasible conjecture with today's knowledge]), Sarah gave birth to Isaac. I could only imagine Abraham's joy as he watched Isaac grow (sadly, for some reason, Ishmael was sent away).

Satan's argumentm which eventually affected Isaac, probably would have gone like this: "Well, God, I just don't understand things sometimes. Why do you have faith in the miserable little creatures made of water and dirt? What has mud ever done for you but cause you headaches? You would be willing to sacrifice everything, and you know that to restore their original state, you will have to do just that, but man wouldn't do the same for you. Just give up, and let us go back to the good old days."

God didn't buy into this, though, and he, unlike Satan, knows the heart of every individual, although Satan has a good idea based on our actions. What sometimes isn't visible to others, even a brilliant, powerful being like Satan, God sees clearly (both good and bad).

So Satan probably went before God and rolled the dice with this question, and the dice came up *Abraham*. Abraham was indeed willing to sacrifice his son, for he knew God had made him an ironclad promise that he'd have a son and that his descendants who would be like the sand and stars in number. He knew Isaac (the second son, just as Jesus was the second perfect man birthed) was his promise fulfilled, and if needed, God could and would raise Isaac from the dead. Abraham killed so many arguments concerning what man was capable of believing if only he was able to grasp and cling to a five-letter word called faith.

We all know the story of Abraham taking Isaac to be sacrifice to God and of his being unwavering in executing God's will, even to the point his arm was drawn in the act of slaying his beloved Isaac. I have three sons and couldn't imagine his heart at that very moment. Then, miracle of miracles (up to that time in history), an angel appeared, stopped Abraham, and provided an alternative sacrifice (an ancient metaphor of Jesus in that it was a ram). God always provides the means to answer any test.

Now about the angel, who was he? The Bible doesn't say, but he was a guardian angel. Satan and many angels were to assist in our becoming what God desired and what brought about the need for the big bang and, therefore, creation. They were, after our creation, always supposed to minister to us in helping us become good, maturing children in the family God had never possessed—children who, like only God, were triune.

After the fall, one-third of angels rebelled and worked against the guardian angels in this endeavor, while two-thirds, being the guardians, worked toward this goal. This is why the world is in turmoil and has been since mankind's fall. For as Paul wrote, "We wrestle not against flesh and blood, but against principalities, against powers, against the rulers of the darkness of this world, against spiritual wickedness in high places."

A word of warning: many today are in danger of angel worshipping. Throughout scripture, there are accounts of man and angels meeting. Many times, the angels would admonish the frightened men, usually prostrate, not to worship them. They are not our lords and do not act according to our whims. They know us pretty well and know doing so would be against our spiritual growth.

Only one being, a man, was worshipped by man and accepted it without offering admonishment. That man was crucified for doing so. But he too had a father who knew resurrection was not beyond the ability of, say, someone who could usher the big bang and the universe into existence. Nothing can come from nothingness. You call the originator of *is*-ness a puzzle (you have no answer). He calls himself I Am (a concept I find hard for ancient man to develop on his own), and I use only three letters to call him—God. Think what you like, but we got here somehow.

WHAT'S LOVE GOT TO DO WITH IT (DNA SWAPPING)?

The first paragraph or two is a bit to chew, but it is short and leads to some interesting thoughts. Jump through this hoop, and the rest of the stroll will be fun.

The definition of *genome* is the ordering of genes in a haploid set of chromosomes of a particular organism, or the full DNA sequence of an organism; "the human genome contains approximately three billion chemical base pairs." In modern molecular biology, the genome is the entirety of an organism's hereditary information. It is encoded either in DNA or, for many types of viruses, in RNA. Genome researchers look at many different features when comparing genomes: sequence similarity, gene location, the length and number of coding regions (called exons) within genes, the amount of noncoding DNA in each genome, and highly conserved regions maintained in organisms as simple as bacteria and as complex as humans. Trying to write this in a manner everyone will understand is a bit complicated, but basically, it is the sequencing of each individual's DNA strands that determine our individual characteristics.

Hair color, eye color, skin color, and body type are physically observable evidence of DNA structure commonality or difference.

Temperament, intelligence, and on and on are (to a degree) non-visibly observable evidence of DNA commonality or difference. This is why, when you walk into a crowded room, you will see many different features distinguishing each individual, which enables us to tell each other apart.

Only identical twins have identically sequenced DNA strands. The more varied the DNA sequencing, the greater the differences between each individual (to a degree, for the physical appearance of one child might more closely match the parent with whom they share the least common sequencing due to their having more in common in unobservable characteristic sequencing commonalities). Now that we've covered that, let's get back to regular English.

Animals and plants and even primitive microorganisms share much common DNA-sequencing structure. The closer we are in appearance, the more DNA commonality we share. When I speak of DNA commonality, I am speaking of commonality between protein-producing genes. Many of the genes in the human genome produce no proteins and were once thought of as "junk DNA," but we are now learning some, if not all, do have functions we do not understand completely. Genes producing protein determine much more than just the appearance of the plant, animal, or microorganism.

In humans, when growth is needed, a certain gene produces more of its protein, which in turn stimulates increased hormonal production when needed (puberty). The pituitary gland, thyroid gland, and adrenal gland all produce growth hormones, and in the disease called gigantism, we see the results when growth-hormone production runs amok. Still, this enables us to understand a man would need greater protein production from a gene (or genes) controlling growth than would mice.

Despite these great differences we see between species, we share a great deal in common with all other life-forms on earth. There is more than 95-98 percent similarity between related genes in humans and apes in general while the similarities between mouse and human genes range from about 70 to 90 percent, with an average of 85 percent similarity but with a lot of variation from gene to gene. Why the genetic similarities between all life on earth?

God's mind is not our mind, and his ways are not our ways. He spoke this universe into being with the purpose of creating a vessel able to produce a triune being like him. We like to think of the Bible as being literal in prose when much of it is actually metaphorical. When it says God created the oceans or the landmasses by dividing the oceans from the land, we think he just said it, and *pop*—it happened in one day. But just as the epic concerning post-Adamic humanity has unfolded over several millennia, what makes you think (other than misinterpreting metaphorical as literal) he would do any different in the creation of the universe?

God also uses us to accomplish his will and bring about his plan to completion. We see this in how Jesus told his disciples to preach the gospel. to Surely he could have snapped his fingers and he would already have his desired family. But he doesn't, and he didn't. He, being the creator, desires his creation to be involved, to learn, and to benefit as his plans unfold. This includes the angels.

The Bible is replete with scripture showing or stating the angels' direct involvement in God's plan even on a minute scale (one miracle as opposed to creation would be minute). The archangel, Gabrial was involved in the birth of Christ as he told Mary she was favored in the yees of God, and would give birth to the Messiah.. We see how Satan, in defiance of God's will, caused Adam and Eve to sin. We see in Genesis how an angel with a sword was placed to guard the entrance to the Garden of Eden after Adam and Eve were expelled. Psalms speaks of angels encamping around servants of God. The prophet Elisha prayed the Lord would open the eyes of his servant so he could see the mighty angelic army of God protecting them. Angels shut the lion's mouth when Daniel was thrown in the lion's den. Angels ministered to Jesus when he was in the Garden of Gethsemane. Paul (Ephesians 3:10) and Peter (1 Peter 1:12) both said the angels eagerly watch us and learn.

I've always believed in an unchanging God. Why then would he do any differently before the creation of Adam? The answer is he didn't. The angels were involved in the creation story up to Adam's creation and are still working hard to see God's plan come to fruition even as a war is waged to thwart God's plan. Since Adam, however, man is also involved in bringing the end result about. In man, you have Satan's children (mostly unaware) battling God's children in a spiritual war. I spoke of this earlier by citing Ephesians 6:12:

[12] We wrestle not against flesh and blood, but against principalities, against powers, against the rulers of the darkness of this world, against spiritual wickedness in high places.

Before Adam, the angels went about doing God's will on a day-to-day basis without knowing what they were doing other than knowing they were simply doing God's will. How, you may ask, can I confidently make the last statement? This is how Jesus instructed us concerning our service in his kingdom. He admonishes us to "take no thought of tomorrow, for today has enough evil therein." If we really trust God has our best interest in heart, it simplifies life greatly, for we can concentrate on the task at hand without worrying about any distractions, or what the outcome will be, as we know God's will is perfect. Goe is the measure and judge of perfection.

Satan worked towards insuring God's will was fulfilled until he was flabbergasted by an unforeseen event—Adam's creation. Until then, he was busy helping in the creation of the great life process as it unfolded over eons. Somehow, the angels, at God's behest, enabled dirt and water to come together and stimulate the process leading to life. Because it was at God's behest, Genesis gives total credit to God in Genesis, chapter one.

Adam, in Genesis, is said to be made of dust of the ground. That is a metaphor for where man himself arose through countless eons of refinement in DNA structuring as unwanted traits were removed and wanted traits (through genetic mutations) were added until one creature (Adam) could reason sufficiently. This enabled God to breathe his Spirit into humanity (which had already existed), incurring the wrath of the being that had worked hard as God's first-in-command to bring about the very being who would supplant him, thus causing him to rebel.

God's plan, since the most primitive life-form arose from some primordial soup, has always been to usher in another set of triune beings who would be like he is in nature. It is estimated that the first life-forms on earth were primitive one-celled creatures that appeared about three billion years ago.

Since that time, angels have been busy (some of them anyway) with the duty of DNA sequencing on a grand scale. They still are doing this, I believe. God saw something unique in Adam's DNA and knew he was desirable for God's purpose. Still, Adam had to be willingly obedient to God's calling. Perhaps this is why Jesus said, "Many are called, but few are chosen." God saw something in Abraham he liked and called Abraham. Abraham answered in obedience and became chosen, and his DNA was passed on through two children who are now at each other's throats.

Satan too can read DNA. Why would he not want Abraham's children in his service? And if he could cause God to lie (God promised Abraham's children would continue in perpetuity), God would be a liar and no longer all-powerful. God's very character and his sinless nature would be destroyed. Satan would have won, for scripture repetitively calls the Jewish people chosen.

The Egyptians, Philistines, Assyrians, Persians, Babylonians, Romans, Hitler, numerous other nations, and now virtually every nation in the Mideast has tried to destroy Israel, and many still are trying. World opinion, by-in-large, is very anti-Israeli. Why would so many throughout many centuries seek to destroy a single people, and how has one tiny nation defied such odds? No other nation has vanished for almost two millennia only to return to the very spot where their ancestors had lived. Could the gene pool have something to do with it? Is it not a gene pool both God and Satan desired and is still central to the plans of both?

Consider the birthplace of Adam. The Middle East is unique in its geographical location. Here, all the races (Negroid, Caucasoid, and Mongoloid) have historically come closest to intersecting geographically. Here would be the place where those with the greatest DNA variations would come together and choose mates with more divergent structures. Here, Michael, as described in Bartholomew 4, could get soil and water (DNA) from people from all over the world or the "four corners" as described. Here, he also found the original Abraham og Genesis, who provided two sons through whom he could pass his genetic material, which apparently pleased both God and Satan. I am not saying all believers in Islam are evil, for they merely haven't come to the light.

As I wrote earlier, God judges us according to our knowledge—for, as Jesus said, "To whom much is given, much is expected." I leave the Almighty to judge all according to what they believe to be true. Only he knows how someone never really given the truth (as I see it, hoping I am not wrong) are judged when, other than their religion, they would be considered saints. However, there are two sides now (one Isaac's descendants, the other Ishmael's) at each other's throats. One being, because of an ancient promise to Abraham, is in charge of one group in accordance to God's will, and the other being, Satan, is leading Ishmael's children. Both sides (as all are to some degree) are confused about their place in God's unfolding plan, yet member of both faith are sure they follow the truth. Soon, things are going to heat up, but again, I digress.

All this genetic monitoring and such continued. At one point, it seemed Saul was the chosen one, but he fell out of grace. Perhaps he had what it took to be called, but his rebellious disobedience after being made king of Israel led to his *not* being chosen (called but not chosen). So God called another with the right stuff—David, who passed from being called to being chosen. His stuff was so right God could, quite a few generations later, put his master plan together and defeat his ancient nemesis, Satan, forever.

A being without Adam's curse—since it was Adam who abdicated his throne, not Eve—was needed. So God chose a descendant of Adam, Abraham, David, and Solomon, on down to Mary, as a vessel to place his Son in. Here in Christ was the first human without the stain of original sin since Adam and Eve bit the metaphorical apple.

Addendum: Upon in-depth research of scripture I have come to realize God didn't use the lineage that went through Solomon, but rather choose one of David's other sons, Nathan, to insure his promise to David that the Messiah would come from his bloodline. The reason God rejected Solomon is he chooose to intermarry with those who worshipped foreign gods when doing such was in direct contradiction of Jewish Law. Because of this the twelve tribes turned from God so much that the nation split into two kingdoms, Israel, and Judah. This is where the term Jew comes from, for when this term originated, Israel had ceased to be. The wages of sin are – death; here the wage paid was the death of any chance it could pass through Solomon, and the death of the nation, Israel. And to think Solomon was the wisest man to ever draw breath. Also, I think it important to note I shall delve much deeper into the thought we are judged guilty of only those thing one did while having knowledge the actions were actually wrong. in a later addendum. In it I shall explain in detail as I give several verses in support of this contention, as I believe strongly in cross references; even when a verse or verses are unambiguous. (end addendum)

It had taken many years for an answer to Adam's willful disobedience. Satan, because none of us are privy to God's plans, was shocked to realize he had made a grand mistake when he had a man without sin put to death. By causing a sinless Adam to transgress, Satan had Adam come under the penalty of death as God had said, "You shall not eat of the fruit of the tree that is in the midst of the garden, neither shall you touch it, lest you die." Death was the penalty for sin. Death, in essence, is eternal separation from God, for we still exist after passing through the veil that is death. This I know due to having spent four days in a coma, thus I speak from first-hand experience. Hell is more horrible than you can begin to imagine.

Using lies and temptation Satan caused Adam's death and fall. Thus, he wrested control of humanity from God, as Adam willingly switched his allegiance. Jesus, because he had no earthly father, had no original sin (passed down from Adam).

In causing a sinless Jesus to die, though he knew not sin, Satan really messed up, for he had no right to kill the innocent or sinless. When Satan did this, he created a situation he couldn't argue himself out of and broke God's law concerning death being the penalty for sin. Where there was no sin, there was no concurring penalty of death, nor could it justifiably be administered. In crucifying Jesus (a hideous death), Satan abrogated his lordship of earth suddenly and for all time, but most Christians do not understand this present reality. This was God's plan as described in 2 Corinthians 5:21:

[21] For He made Him who knew no sin to be sin for us, that we might become the righteousness of God in Him.

The only thing incumbent for each individual is we must realize our true state (sinners) and recognize the price has been paid for our sins, accept both as truth, repent, and ask to become what God has always wanted, or what all creation came into existence to provide, a member of a growing family. You can do so right now by telling Jesus you believe he died on the cross for your sins, repent of your sins, believe he arose from the dead, and ask him to be your Lord and Savior. It is as simple as it is marvelously mysterious – so mysterious is caught all but a few of the Nation of Judah off guard.

The plan is still unfolding, and I am sure, God is monitoring our DNA. What is God looking for? Has it already happened? Is there someone who unknowingly possesses what God is looking for, and he is calling, but they refuse to join the ranks of the chosen? Could that someone be you, for although I believe all can come to God, all are not capable of doing certain tasks? Could you be the one whom God could use to usher in Christ's return, or will God have to choose someone else when the time arises? Beware the act of disobedience should you be called.

If God is calling you and you will not answer, he will call someone else. This is made clear in Esther 4:14 when Mordecai says to Esther,

[14] For if thou altogether holdest thy peace at this time, then shall there enlargement and deliverance arise to the Jews from another place; but thou and thy father's house shall be destroyed: and who knoweth whether thou art come to the kingdom for such a time as this?

Jesus said, "My kingdom is not of this world." Who knows whether you are being called to his kingdom for just such a time as this?

God is searching the world over for faithful servants (family members). This is made clear in 2 Chronicles 16:9:

[9] For the eyes of the LORD run to and fro throughout the whole earth, to show himself strong in the behalf of them whose heart is perfect toward him.

God is a great wheel that can't be stopped. You can climb aboard and become a being our minds cannot begin to fathom, or you can resist and end up being crushed. Resistance is futile. In every country, corporation, human family, pack of animals, sports team, you name it—there is ultimately one (and only one) person able to display the logo stating "The buck stops here."

I, for one, would prefer to follow the true Supreme Being rather than he who tried to garner supremacy by causing the spiritual death of my first ancestor in the Adamic line chosen by God. Since Adam, Satan has despised mankind and he's done everything to destroy it; from each individual to the race as a whole.

The train that began its run billions of years ago when the universe was created is nearing a point where things are going to change drastically. Are you on board or stuck on the tracks and tied down by the encumbrances provided for and stoked by Satan and his followers, which are: "[16] For all that is in the world, the lust of the flesh, and the lust of the eyes, and the pride of life, is not of the Father, but is of the world" (1 John 2:16)?

I covered more than I intended. Bouncing from such complex scientific information to a yet-blazed theological trail is more than tiring. If I made any mistakes, please let me know.

THIS EA RTHEN VESSEL

David wrote in Psalm 8:3-5 three verses that perhaps all thinking men and women have contemplated when observing the vastness of the night sky with its myriad shimmering stars spread across a sprawling pitch-black canvas. In it, he pondered this question:

[3] When I consider thy heavens, the work of thy fingers, the moon and the stars, which thou hast ordained;

[4] What is man, that thou art mindful of him? and the son of man, that thou visitest him?

[5] For thou hast made him a little lower than the angels, and hast crowned him with glory and honour.

David recognized that man, above all other creatures on earth, held a special place in the eyes of the Originator, but why would God hold us above every other earthly creature? What is his purpose? What is *our* purpose, and who is ultimately responsible for bringing our purpose to fruition? Some pretty deep questions to consider. I love how David stated that God visited us. Has he visited you lately? He wishes to.

In spite of man's special place in creation, all Christians (as well as Jews and Muslims) believe man arose from the same source—dust or dirt. Genesis says this, while the Gospel of Bartholomew says, "Earth from the four ends of the world and water from the four rivers of Paradise [there were four rivers in the Garden of Eden]." Christians believing in evolution (if there are any besides me) believe man also arose from earth and water in some type of primordial soup, as I explained earlier. Those believing in either supposition (creationism or evolution) both believe man is, in effect, an earthen vessel created for a particular purpose. But the question is, what purpose?

Addendum: I want to again reiterate my stressing of the Gospel of Bartholomen in no way means it has stood the scrutiny that was used by early Church fathers who arrived to the conclusion it met the standards needed to become canonized. It didn't for good reasons. However, I found it interesting a source other than canonized scripture confirms what is said in Genesis 2:7.

In answering the question as to why we exist, I would like to consider a piece of scripture where Jeremiah, speaking on the Originator's behalf, uses pure metaphor that is undeniable as far as nation being an earthen vessel made for the Originator's purpose. Read Jeremiah 18:1-6,

[1] The word which came to Jeremiah from the LORD, saying,

[2] Arise, and go down to the potter's house, and there I will cause thee to hear my words.

[3] Then I went down to the potter's house, and, behold, he wrought a work on the wheels.

[4] And the vessel that he made of clay was marred in the hand of the potter: so he made it again another vessel, as seemed good to the potter to make it.

[5] Then the word of the LORD came to me, saying,

[6] O house of Israel, cannot I do with you as this potter? saith the LORD. Behold, as the clay is in the potter's hand, so are ye in mine hand, O house of Israel.

Now supplant the words "house of Israel" with your name, for he does with each individual as did he with Israel. As I have said, it doesn't matter whether you believe in a seven-day creation or evolution, so long as you're honest in professing what you really believe. Nowhere in the Bible does it say all scripture must be taken literally (it shouldn't), yet many try to do just that and do so with the best of intentions, believing such to be the truth. Should they profess otherwise, they are liars. The church once condemned Galileo and Copernicus as being apostates for saying the solar system and even the universe was not Earth-centered.

It was the Protestant churches, with their fundamentalist views on the sole authority of the scripture, that took the lead by launching a barrage of attacks on Copernicus and his ideas. These were great men of God who led many to Christ, and who got so much right where salvation is concerned.

John Calvin (1509-1564) was the father of Calvinism. Many modern denominations that are held in high regard, and that have millions of followers worldwide base much of their dogma on Calvinism. Calvin, as did the leaders of all denominations in existence at that time, lent his voice to this condemnation and cried out, "Who will venture to place the authority of Copernicus above that of the Holy Spirit?"

Martin Luther (1483-1546) joined in this harsh criticism against Copernicus, calling him "an upstart astrologer" and "a fool." Luther's condemnation was based on the authority of the Bible as he understood it, for he said,

"This is how things go nowadays. Anyone who wants to be clever must not let himself like what others do. He must produce his own product as this man (Copernicus) does, who wishes to turn the whole of astronomy upside down. But I believe in the Holy Scripture, since Joshua ordered the Sun, not the earth to stand still."

Luther's disciple Melanchthon (1497-1560) had this to add;

"Now it is in want of honesty to assert such notions publicly, and the example is pernicious. It is part of a good mind to accept the truth as revealed by God and to acquiesce to it."

The Catholic Church was no different, as it forced Galileo to recant his assertions of a heliocentric solar system and even burned some at the stake for not recanting such assertions. Few sins are more egregious than murdering someone in a horrible manner for simply expressing what they believe to be true. Galileo spent the remainder of his life under house arrest after making assertions the solar system was heliocentric even though he'd recanted such assertions.

People had always believed, based on scripture and observation, the earth was indeed the center of all things. To say you believed otherwise, unless you were one of the very few, highly educated scientists living when this idea was first postulated, would have been dishonest. Professing otherwise was a leap few could make based on their life experiences or the teaching of the theologians of that time period.

Still, God has always known the reality of it all and did not consider those believing an untruth to be malicious sinners because they postulated a lie (although punishing anyone for their beliefs is inexcusable, for punishment of beliefs is the purview of God alone). The Originator is a being of unadulterated truth, and as science reveals his mysteries, we will come to understand some things, like the Earth-centered universe, are not true. I am not saying scripture is untrue, for using metaphor, scripture was able to explain extremely complex concepts in a manner early man would otherwise not comprehend at all. When scripture is dealing with historical facts, names of individuals, and commandments written unambiguously, we accept it as being literal in nature.

We humans in general, those professing various religious views in particular, seem to find special delight in stressing that which separates, or splinters, us. We love to prove our dogmatic interpretations to all be correct, and many go through great extremes to do so. With this mindset. we nitpick the smallest issues and find great delight in doing so. In doing so, we drive others away instead of drawing them to the light with patience, compassion, and love. This sad state of affairs began almost immediately after Christ's ascension into heave shortly after dying, for Paul bemoans the fracturing of the Body of Christ (Church) in 1st Corinthians 1:10-13:

10 I appeal to, brothers and sisters, in the name of our Lord Jesus Christ, that all of you agree with one another in what you say

and that there be no divisions among you, but that you be perfectly united in mind and thought.

11 My brothers and sisters, some from Chloe's household have informed me that there are quarrels among you.

12 What I mean is this: One of you says, "I follow Paul"; another, "I follow Apollos"; another, "I follow Cephas "; still another, "I follow Christ."

13 Is Christ divided? Was Paul crucified for you? Were you baptized in the name of Paul?

I am not admonishing that you compromise your beliefs, but if they are strong enough, it's your lifestyle, and the signs and miracles tha accompany every Christians life, not your mouth, that should be what reaches others and shows them what the Originator really desires of us. Many people become pharisaical (I had to look that one up) in the way they treat unbelievers and even other believers. In essence, those who would be chosen become like those who crucified Christ by placing unnecessary burdens on true believers, which could (and often do) cause them to stumble. In this, something is amiss.

Adam, when he was created, had the breath of God breathed into him, after which he became a living soul (Genesis 2:7). What exactly does this mean? And what is God's plan? It is revealed in Genesis when he cursed the serpent by saying in Genesis 3:15,

[15] And I will put enmity between thee and the woman, and between thy seed (those not answering the call to salvation) and her seed (those answering the call); it (Christ) shall bruise thy head, and thou shalt bruise his heel.

Words in parenthesis in the scripture above were interjected by me to help you understand. God's plan was to undo the state of contamination that Satan, through sin, foisted upon all realms of reality. Even heaven itself was contaminated, for Satan, at times, has an audience with God (how often, I don't know), as seen in Job.

Consider how in Satan and his angelic followers—pure, sinless beings with near absolute knowledge of their Creator—became corrupt and, in doing so, corrupted all creation. Remember how I wrote earlier that God, several times in scripture, is called the balancer of scales and how he hates a false scale (sin)? Well, through man, God is able to set the scales straight once again—forever.

Adam is the progenitor of all potential Spirit-filled humanity. This is why Jesus is called "son of man" in the New Testament. I used the word "potential Spirit filled" due to the fact we, man, are not born possessing the Holy Spirit, as were Adam and Eve, for their sin of rebellion caused God's Spirit to depart from their being. Christ has made the return of this original state, the Holy Spirit (the breath of life) a reality for any and all who accept the sacrifice Christ made when dying a horrible death on the cross.

God's plan was so marvelous, no one save a few prophets throughout the ages saw it coming, and even they didn't understand it completely. Because of Satan's treachery, we post-Adamic humans (sons and daughters of man) come to the Originator in a state of complete ignorance and steeped in sin—the exact opposite of what Satan and the fallen angels were before they rebelled. Our being imperfect, yet accepting of God in this state (ignorant) enables God to rebalance the scales sent out of kilter by the fallen angels (once perfect and with perfect knowledge). If that isn't a balancing of the scales act, I do not know what might be.

But what was Adam's original state? Was his fleshly body meant to exist forever in the state in which he was born? Genesis 2:17 might shed some light on this question:

But of the tree of the knowledge of good and evil, thou shalt not eat of it: for in the day that thou eatest thereof thou shalt surely die.

Now on the other side (after death), we will, like Christ, have bodies, making us truly triune, but they will be different after being transfigured, for Jesus was able to walk through a door after being raised and transfigured.

It is plain to see here the Originator saw two life forces in Adam and Eve. One was each's physical body and soul the other; each one's spirit. God stated both Adam and Eve would die the very day they too tasted that metaphorical fruit (sin). Satan had already tempted one-third of angels to eat of that forbidden fruit when they changed their allegiance from God to Satan.

The serpent, as he'd done with the now fallen angels, caused Eve to sin. I am sure he tempted them with the offer of a promotion if only they switched sides and followed him. He did the same with Eve. She believed Satan's lie she would become like him and and the other fallen angels, thus in turn caused Adam to sin. Those thinking of Eve as the weak one here should think again, for she took the initiative and led Adam to do the same. In this Adam was a follower, not man enough to own up to his own failings. Had he not followed Eve, I believe God could have, and would have, created another Eve, for the necessary material (DNA) was first found in Adam.

Addendum: If you find it surprising hearing the forbidden fruit was literally Adam and Eve's changing allegiance from God to Satan, I did a deep dive into the meaning of Genesis 3:5 and discovered it hinged on two words in that verse:

1. Did Satan say God knew she'd become like God, or the gods, for some versions (most modern) read Gods, while many older versions say the gods (with a small g). It makes all the difference, for if he, as I believe it should read, says the gods, Satan was telling her he would become like the fallen angels, who were magnificent looking, as you shall see in a future addendum.
2. The second word that led to my concluding a switch in allegiance was the metaphorical "apple" is nachash. Nachash has three different meanings; much like English words often sound the same, but have various meanings. Nachash means serpent, to work divination, and it also means bright like the sun shining on highly polished brass. When you read Ezekiel 28:13, it becomes apparent why she would want to be like him: 13 You were in Eden, the garden of God; Every precious stone *was* your covering: The sardius, topaz, and diamond, Beryl, onyx,

and jasper, Sapphire, turquoise, and emerald with gold. The workmanship of your timbrels and pipes Was prepared for you on the day you were created. (end addendum)

I find it fascinating God says Adam and Eve would die the day they partook of the forbidden fruit, yet they didn't die physically. Rather, they lived until old age (hundreds of years) and gave birth to offspring. Also, there were other humans present as they raised their family, for Cain feared punishment from men elsewhere for killing Abel. There is so much that, if you think about it logically, doesn't line up with scripture as it has been and is taught, for our understanding has increased due to scientific advances—remember Copernicus.

Adam and Eve were spiritually alive due to their being filled with Holy Spirit, but they ended up being like those Jesus speaks of in Luke 8:13, but to give you the whole context as to what Jesus is speaking of, I would like to give you verses 11, 12, 14, and 15, also that we all may assess where we are spiritually according to these verses.

Luke 8:11-15 [11] "This is what the parable means: the seed is the word of God. [12] The seeds that fell along the path stand for those who hear; but the Devil comes and takes the message away from their hearts in order to keep them from believing and being saved. [13] The seeds that fell on rocky ground stand for those who hear the message and receive it gladly. But it does not sink deep into them; they believe only for a while but when the time of testing comes, they fall away. [14] The seeds that fell among thorn bushes stand for those who hear; but the worries and riches and pleasures of this life crowd in and choke them, and their fruit never ripens. [15] The seeds that fell in good soil stand for those who hear the message and retain it in a good and obedient heart, and they persist until they bear fruit.

Adam and Eve died the instant they sinned, but the death was spiritual in nature. They were akin to those just beginning their walk with Christ. Those just beginning to walk in the Christian faith need to hear the word preached in sermons, and they need to read it that they may mature as spiritual beings. There was no scripture when Adam and Eve lived, so the angels were to assist them in their spiritual journey, except because of jealousy Lucifer changed his character and became Satan that he might overthrow God, while destroying humanity – the object of his eternal ire. And to think some worship him.

The Holy Spirit inhabits the body the moment one is saved. It inhabited Adam and Eve the moment God breathed the breath of life into them, as seen in Genesis 2:7: *7 And the Lord God formed man of the dust of the ground, and breathed into his nostrils the breath of life; and man became a living soul.*

Those not saved (reborn of the Spirit) are not alive spiritually speaking. This Jesus tells us in Luke 9:60 when he tells a potential follower who wanted to bury his father to "let the dead bury the dead, and instead go forth and spread the gospel".

Humanity is in it's current state because God cannot abide sin, as we read in Habakkuk 1:13: "Your eyes are too pure to look on evil" (CSB).

God had such grand plans for humanity, but Adam and Eve disobeyed God, which is the very definition of sin. God knew immediately, for what parent doesn't know when their child dies?

You may ask how I arrived at this conclusion. Only knowledge of scripture (I have a doctorate in theology, which I'm now unable to use in the pulpit, so I write) has enabled me to do so, along with prayer. As I said before, God is unchanging. He doesn't change, and his plans do not change. Think of God's master plan as a clay vessel being formed on the potter's wheel. When it became warped with sin, what would God, the master potter, do? Would he scrap his plan? Far from it. He would simply rework the clay on the spinning wheel and, being the Originator, continue on with his plan. What then is his plan?

Consider 1 Peter 1:20,

[20] Who (Christ) verily was foreordained before the foundation of the world, but was manifest in these last times for you.

We see God's plan hasn't changed since before the foundation of the world (before Adam). God's plan was the same before the earth was created and certainly before Adam was created.

Let's look at 1 Peter 1:23:

[23] Being born again, not of corruptible seed, but of incorruptible, by the word of God, which liveth and abideth for ever.

We see that, once again, God is able to (as was always his plan) plant his seed, which is God's word. Upon becoming saved, God puts the Holy Spirit in man again. Once more man is, as were Adam and Eve before the fall, alive, for the redeemed become, as Jesus calls it in the Gospels – born again.

But there is a vast difference between Adam's original state (it was corruptible), and the state of those born again, The Word of God is incorruptible. The first chapter of the gospel of John tells us Jesus is the Word. Adam and Eve didn't have scripture, which is inspired by the Word, thus God used angels to teach them, whereas we have the word.

Some of the angels God entrusted with teaching Adam and Eve as to how to grow and understand spiritual truths corrupted themselves. The seed planted in them died when they who had not known sin became a casualty of sin, and sadly the penalty is death.

Those born again, according to Peter, are incorruptible. If you disagree I have no problem with that, for I believe we should all live as if incorruptibility isn't a fact, therefore giving us no reason to think we are able to, or should, stray from our purpose. Incorruptibility is what I believe, and I respect your belief, for it isn't a major difference inhibiting one from accepting the seed according to God's plan. As believers, you will be judged only according to what you do with the seed planted in you. This is why we are referred to as a living temple of God.

Addendum: I am now ambivalent concerning the belief "once saved, always saved". None will be one hundred percent sure unless they'd heard it straight from God's mouth. I hope it's true, for some I love, believing this, act as if they are free to sin without consequence. But Paul spoke of running the race to the end in reference to being saved, and Jesus speaks of the seed that was planted (born again), came up, but the weeds (sinful lifestyles) choked its life out. (end addendum)

I find comfort in the fact that if we do mess up, the Originator merely begins to rework the vessel, for if we repent he does not throw it (us) away any more than he threw Israel away. Punishment, though, always follows disobedience as seen in Jewish history, scripture, and as explained by Paul in Hebrews 12:7-8:

[7] If ye endure chastening, God dealeth with you as with sons; for what son is he whom the father chasteneth not?

[8] But if ye be without chastisement, whereof all are partakers, then are ye bastards, and not sons.

If you answer the call, it behooves you to walk the walk, rather talk the talk. And do so not just to avoid punishment, for then you are fighting a defensive battle.

The real reason to be as obedient as possible is to unlock the realm of possibility that opens when you take on your new nature. The moment you accept your purpose, righteous angels become your ministering agents, but that isn't the greatest benefit. The greatest benefit is the unimaginable power that makes us members of God's family. His Holy Spirit, that which connects us in much the same manner blood connects family members, is poured into the believer, thereby uniting all believers with the Godhead. In this manner, God's plan unfolds perfectly (as should all things when an all-powerful being is involved).

Through humanity (in the form of Jesus), all entities that corrupted are defeated. Humanity is able to bridge the gap between fallen man and God, and the Originator is able to resume his original plan whereby God seeds a family of triune beings.

Pretty awesome, but it gets even better, for someday, because of the fulfillment of this plan, all vestiges of sin will be removed from our existence as described in Revelation 20:13-15:

[13] And the sea gave up the dead which were in it; and death and hell delivered up the dead which were in them: and they were judged every man according to their works.

[14] And death and hell were cast into the lake of fire. This is the second death.
[15] And whosoever was not found written in the book of life was cast into the lake of fire.
Literally, it is a hell of a price to pay for those who willingly and with ample knowledge refuse to accept a gift of such great value and sacrifice, which is so graciously offered. Sadly, sin was never to be part of the Originator's plan, but now, after Adam's fall and Christ's redeeming death and resurrection, it became just a few-thousand-year sidetrack, causing the Originator to rework the clay symbolizing his plan.
This is it for today. I may take tomorrow off, for this—the research and thought involved in bringing these ideas together—is a bit overwhelming.
Hopefully, though, I will be refreshed come tomorrow. I think I will next explore the difference between the living and the dead (as in the walking dead). Thanks.
—Sam
PS: I freely share this with the world. Anyone claiming this as his or her own does so at their own peril even if you do not believe in an Originator. It is my belief the scales would be set out of kilter as far as you are concerned. Just a friendly warning.

THE GIFT OF PROPHECY

When you become familiar with the Old Testament and the stories involving the many prophets God sent to deal with Israel, you might ask yourself, "Why in the world do they call prophecy a "gift"?"

Prophets have always arisen from among true believers of the Originator. Satan, too, has his prophets, and we see some using this gift for gain, something God forbids his followers from doing. Most fortune tellers are charlatans, but a few have a gift and they use it to make money telling friends and strangers, alike, what the future may hold in store; all for a price. This is strictly forbidden by scripture.

God's prophets were messengers often delivering cryptic messages even they themselves did not understand unless it dealt with an individual or with an individual circumstance (like Samuel choosing Saul, then David to be king of the Jewish nation), or unless God explained the meaning.

Dreams were often a form of prophecy, like when Joseph had two dreams indicating he would have a position someday wherein he would rise to prominence over them. They hated him for this, and sold him into slavery; the very thing that enabled his dreams to come true.

Proving he uses whomever he wishes to accomplish his desire,

God even sent dreams to individuals who were not prophets so prophets could decipher the meaning, as seen when Joseph explained to Pharoah the meaning of his frightening dream.

Another example is God sent Nebuchadnezzer a dream about a giant statue made of various metals, which so frightened him he offered great wealth to anyone who could decipher it. As God did with Pharoah by sending Joseph, a man of God to interpret his dream, God sent Daniel to convey the meaning of of Nebuchadnezzer's cryptic dream.

Note in both cases a man of God was, end the end, the one delivering the prophecy. Both rulers were instruments of power and authority God used to accomplish his desire. They suited God's purpose.

Still, when all is said and done, God uses his prophets to reveal and confirm things to come so his chosen ones (saints of all ages)) will be forewarned, for he would not have us caught off guard as Satan plots against us (now, the Church). Prophets primary purpose was, is, and will be to channel mankind into God's fulfilling purpose, and in doing so creating those who are called saints.

Various individuals during the early periods of scripture were prophets (Enoch, Methuselah, and Noah were prophets). Following the antediluvian period, the descendants of Abraham was the pool of individuals from which God chose his prophets' all chosen that we, his offspring, might know what lies ahead. This continued until Christ was born.

Many wonder if prophecy is still relevant after the lives of the apostles chosen by Jesus (Paul included). We shall discuss this near the end of today's writing, but I digress.

I'd like to break down and explain who the progenitors of God's Old Testament prophets were.

The progenitors of God's Old Testament prophets lived during the antediluvian period (time before Noah's flood). Enoch, Methuselah, and Noah, all being prophets, lived during this two thousand year span of time. Noah was the last antideluvian prophet, for the flood insured that to be.

Noah, after surviving the flood, lived for quite a while. While he yet lived, a man was born named Abraham. The two were contemporaries for thirty-nine years.

Abraham, his child, Isaac, one of his two grandchildren, Jacob, and all twelve of Jacob's children became known as the patriarchs; the eponymous progenitors of the twelve tribes of Israel. God chose his prophets, minor and major, from the twelve tribes, each fathered by one of Abraham's great grandchildren.

Because of the famine during the time of Joseph (Abraham's great grandson son), the descendants of Abraham moved to Egypt and spent just over four hundred years there, during which time there was no mention of prophecy. Sometimes, it seems (when prophecy appears to cease) as if God has lost his voice.

Other times, it seems God is screaming. This occurs when great change or a great event is about to happen or is being foretold. When it comes time for something to happen, a prophet always arose at just the right moment.

Prophets were as human as you and I are. The only difference is, by possessing a greater level of faith and obedience, they enabled God use them to a much greater degree than most are willing to do. God is able to use us only to the degree he allow, for he respects our free will.

Moses, one of the greatest prophets ever, was born shortly before it was time for the descendants of Abraham (the Jewish people) to leave Egypt. When Moses went to tell Pharoah to release God's chosen (Jews), Pharoah, believing himself to be God, hardened his heart and refused.

After ten God sent plagues, Pharaoh acquiesced. Anytime something big is about to happen, there will be resistance, for there is occurring a spiritual warfare unlike anything we humans can imagine, and this battle is often (almost always) manifested by earthly conflicts (think of the Mideast right now).

The Book of Judges recounts how in the time after the death of Joshua, but before Israel began to be ruled by a king, there was a line of individuals known as the Judges. They led Israel, often arising during times of conflict and turmoil. This era lasted approximately 200 years, from around 1200 BCE to 1000 BCE.

There were a total of 12 major judges mentioned, including figures like Deborah, Gideon, and Samson. The prophets and judges had no competing political system (kingdom) and wielded a great deal of power (the population feared and respected them). The power they wielded was, by and large, regional. Judges arose during times of peril, and often at the behest of praying believers, with many being military leaders Deborah, and some rogues (Samson). All fulfilled God's will to a degree. The degree was limited by their lack of committal to the cause. Imagine what Samson, with all his strength, could have done had he truly followed God, rather than repenting in the end and going out in a blaze of glory.

As soon as Saul rose to prominence as a king, things changed, for even Samuel had to contend with the new reality when he secretly sought out David, Saul's replacement when God rejected Saul. Still, when Samuel went to David's home to find the new king, the locals were terrified when Samuel showed up unannounced. Both prophets and judges were feared and rejected.

One thread is common concerning all prophets: their calling caused great resistance from dark, powerful spiritual forces. This can be seen by the manner in which the prophets throughout history were treated.

Some were beheaded; others were thrown into a lion's den, or fed into a fiery furnace, or they were buried up to their waist in mud. Some were stoned, some boiled in oil, others crucified right-side. Various others were either upside down, or exiled, or ostracized, or beaten. All were both hated and cursed. If it was on the receiving end of punishment, they pretty much felt it.

One prophet, Hosea, was even asked to marry and stay with a harlot, though Jewish law permitted divorce, so he could better identify with God's relationship with Israel. This was because God felt as if the Jewish nation was an adulterous whore, chasing after the gods of this world, and God was the ever-faithful husband.

Amazing, isn't it, how both Israel and the church are

metaphorically called spouses or brides. Where this is concerned, though, it is much more than metaphor, for a wife gives birth to children. The Hebrew religion, with it written doctrine, as well as the Church which supplanted it, analogous to a wife birthing God's offspring. Both had the written word, or God's seed that followers of both faiths could read or hear the truth, and decide if they would become God's children. This is his only purpose for humanity—to spawn offspring who, like he, are triune.

Now back to the prophets. In the Old Testament, they were under the influence of the Holy Spirit of God in doing their services. This is made clear when Elisha asked for a double portion of the spirit Elijah had possessed.

Although Elijah told him what he asked for was hard, it must have pleased God greatly, for Elisha has twenty-eight miracles attributed to him whereas Elijah has fourteen. Let me be perfectly clear about this, for the Bible is; never will anyone with a rightly unselfish heart and who is asking God to accept them into his service be denied, period. (9/23/24)

However, God might not call you to do what you want, for God will use you according to the talents, also called gifts, you have. He also has a place for anyone no matter what their talent. Furthermore, God is able to bequeath talents you never had, but more often than bequeathing of new talents, he simply reveals gifts you were never aware of.

Still, I think it is incumbent to realize just what you are getting into, for the path, like all seldom-traveled trails, is rough and narrow. But the rewards, not necessarily the visible ones, are unequaled, never-ending, and inexhaustible. There is a sense of purpose you can see in each prophet and an assurance that could only come from their knowing their power source is unmatchable, unyielding, and unending. The prophets were unyielding in quest to be faithful stewards of any gift God gave them for God is omnipotent (all powerful),omniscient (all knowing, and omnipresent (everywhere). Small wonder is left as to why, in the face of incredible persecution, God's unflinching prophets stood firm.

I want to stress strongly that the prophets often had more that one gift bestowed by God upon them. Elijah and Elisha could rasie the dead. Some could stop the rains at God's behest. Danile slept while force to stay in a den full of ravenous lions yet was unharmed. Many are the miracles these prophets performed: some of which are amazing.

Elijah even called fire down from heaven to set afire logs that were totally drenched to burn the sacrifice offered to God , thereby confirming God's existence. This he did to show the prophets of Baal (a popular pagan god) were false prophets, for in a contest between (G)gods (one a upper case G God, one a lower case g god). His sacrifice was miraculously accepted after Baal's false prophets were unable to appease Baal into setting the dry logs they'd place beneath their sacrifice. It didn't end well for the false prophets, for they had led many away from God. Beware the false prophet. Beware the fortune teller, for God's child does not sell the gifts given freely.

The victory of any believer doing God's will is always assured, even in death (most of the twelve apostles)). And death absolutely will not come until his purpose in you is fulfilled. Caleb makes this clear in Joshua 14:10-11:

[10] And now, behold, the LORD hath kept me alive, as he said, these forty and five years, even since the LORD spake this word unto Moses, while the children of Israel wandered in the wilderness: and now, lo, I am this day fourscore and five years old.

[11] As yet I am as strong this day as I was in the day that Moses sent me: as my strength was then, even so is my strength now, for war, both to go out, and to come in.

Eighty-five-year-old Caleb was fearless because he had a purpose greater than himself backed by an all-powerful being. It took over forty years for his faith to bear fruit, but he held firm until it happened. Too often we give up before the task is done. This is why the phrase "Wait upon the Lord" is repeated (especially in Psalms) many times in scripture.

Since it is through the prophets that God speaks and makes

known his message, his concerns, his frustrations, and his plans, what do you think the world says to the prophets? The answer is held in two simple words and an exclamation mark—*shut up*!

Over and over, they tried to still the voices of the prophets. But what drove the prophets to, despite life-threatening opposition, rise up and proclaim God's message? The answer is a quite simple one most never come close to grasping.

The prophets sold out to a purpose and the love of a being far greater than self, for the most miserable individuals are the most selfish, while the most selfless possess a "peace that passeth all understanding" (Philippians 4:7).

Peace of heart cannot be purchased, stolen, conquered, cajoled, worn, consumed, kissed, or gained in any of the myriad ways we see people trying to gain it. It is only an extension of God.

This incredible peace possessed by true, dedicated believers and the prophets is, however, anathema to the world and all unbelievers. Unbelievers respond as the world moves them to, while the prophets of God act as the Spirit of God moves them, so unbelievers try to shut the mouths of those who are the voice of God. This is made clear when the Originator addresses the Jewish nation concerning this matter in Amos 2:11-12:

[11] And I raised up of your sons for prophets, and of your young men for Nazarites. Is it not even thus, O ye children of Israel? saith the LORD.

[12] But ye gave the Nazarites wine to drink; and commanded the prophets, saying, Prophesy not.

It really angers God when someone, anyone, tells him to shut up. And it is through both scripture and prophecy that God has always voiced his will and intentions.

Prophecy was recorded throughout scripture, beginning with Genesis when God told Adam and Eve they'd die if they ate the fruit (some prophecy is conditional) and continued up to and throughout the New Testament. In scripture, prophecy culminates in one book dealing almost specifically with prophecy. This book is known as the book of Revelation or the Apocalypse of John, which is the last book in the Bible. So let's tackle a question central to our times—did prophecy and prophets end with Revelation?

During the early period of the church, the gifts of the Spirit were in full evidence as seen by the various miracles. The gifts are described in 1 Corinthians 12:8-11:

[8] For to one is given by the Spirit the word of wisdom; to another the word of knowledge by the same Spirit;

[9] To another faith by the same Spirit; to another the gifts of healing by the same Spirit;

[10] To another the working of miracles; to another prophecy; to another discerning of spirits; to another divers kinds of tongues; to another the interpretation of tongues:

[11] But all these worketh that one and the selfsame Spirit, dividing to every man severally as he will.

Here, we see these gifts were special—very special—but you do not see them in evidence much, if at all, in today's churches. Have the gifts in evidence of God's will ceased being exhibited, and if so, is this scriptural?

Let us look into the arguments of those who posit the notion that the gifts have ceased in the church. What scripture(s) do they hang their hat on? There are only two or three pieces of scripture used by those arguing the gifts of the Spirit are no longer operating or seen in the church.

The first and most used is found in 1 Corinthians 13:8-12:

[8] Charity never faileth: but whether there be prophecies, they shall fail; whether there be tongues, they shall cease; whether there be knowledge, it shall vanish away.

[9] For we know in part, and we prophesy in part.

[10] But when that which is perfect is come, then that which is in part shall be done away.

[11] When I was a child, I spake as a child, I understood as a child, I thought as a child: but when I became a man, I put away childish things.

[12] For now we see through a glass, darkly; but then face to

face: now I know in part; but then shall I know even as also I am known. ***

The preceding argument that biblical Gifts of the Spirit have ceased hinges on seven words from verse ten above (when that which is perfect has come). Only this verse supports this doctrine when adhered to by those beliening this for this reason. It is dire to build a doctrine based on one verse especially when other verses refute their contention.

One verse that refutes this notion that the gifts have ceased is found only three verses later, in 1st Corinthians 13:12 (see above). This verse begins by stating we now know in part. But it ends by saying, *but when that which is perfect comes, we will know in full* (God possesses one hundred percent knowledge about all/us). Therefore, their interpretation of 1st Cor 13:9 against the Gifts of the Spirit no longer being relevant in today's Christian Church comes to naught for verse twelve totally refutes this idea.

The second scripture I've seen, and this one amazed me, is found is based on the doctrines of a different denomination using the above. It is found in Matthew 7:21-23:

[21] Not every one that saith unto me, Lord, Lord, shall enter into the kingdom of heaven; but he that doeth the will of my Father which is in heaven.

[22] Many will say to me in that day, Lord, Lord, have we not prophesied in thy name? and in thy name have cast out devils? and in thy name done many wonderful works?

[23] And then will I profess unto them, I never knew you: depart from me, ye that work iniquity.

The argument holds even less water, for this argument posits the believers in modern-day gifts of the Spirit are the very ones Jesus was referring to as having never known, but they overlook one thing.

The apostles and other early followers would also have fallen into this category, and certainly, Jesus knew them well. When one goes to scripture trying to prove a point, they sometimes have to twist scripture to their purpose. Any scripture worth its weight in argument will have much more than one example to back their argument as I shall soon show.

Now concerning those supporting the argument for the gifts of the Spirit still being visible (visibility should and will be much more evident soon), I shall lay down several scriptures supporting this contention, for they are easy to find. I used to swing an ax when I was growing up on the farm. When splitting logs, the first strike was the most important, for it, if placed well and hard, made the job so much simpler.

Therefore, I will start with Mark 16:15-18:

[15] And he said unto them, Go ye into all the world, and preach the gospel to every creature.

[16] He that believeth and is baptized shall be saved; but he that believeth not shall be damned.

[17] And these signs shall follow them that believe; In my name shall they cast out devils; they shall speak with new tongues;

[18] They shall take up serpents; and if they drink any deadly thing, it shall not hurt them; they shall lay hands on the sick, and they shall recover.

It says "whosoever believes" and says nothing about these signs ceasing and marvelously dispels the second argument against gifts, which I offered above. My question is, where are these manifestations today, and why do we not see them more often exhibited? Something is amiss in the kingdom of God.

A second scripture, which ties into and supports the first, is 1 Corinthians 1:7-8:

[7] Therefore you do not lack any spiritual gift as you eagerly wait for our Lord Jesus Christ to be revealed.

[8] He will keep you strong to the end, so that you will be blameless on the day of our Lord Jesus Christ.

Here, Paul is telling us we lack no spiritual gift. He is not just talking to individuals, for everyone will not have all gifts (very, very few will), but the Body of Christ (his church) would. Again, when I look around, I see something is amiss in the Body of Christ. It is up to us, as willing and obedient children, to accept what God has planned, and the gifts are a vastly underutilized part of this plan.

Another scripture supporting the case for modern-day evidence of the gifts of the Spirit is John 14:11-12:

[11] Believe me that I am in the Father, and the Father in me: or else believe me for the very works' sake.

[12] Verily, verily, I say unto you, **He** that believeth on me, the works that I do shall he do also; and greater [works] than these shall he do; because I go unto my Father.

He is in boldface because I want it seen plainly that these gifts of the Spirit were to be seen in perpetuity until that which is perfect has come (when Christ returns). I cannot comprehend how anyone could argue otherwise in light of what is penned so plainly.

Two other supporting scriptures are as follows:

[4] God also testified to [our great salvation] by signs, wonders and various miracles, and gifts of the Holy Spirit distributed according to his will. (Hebrews 2:4)

[17] Every good and perfect gift is from above, coming down from the Father of the heavenly lights, who *does not change* like shifting shadows. (italics used for emphasis is mine)

Although I believe this pretty much proves the argument in favor of modern-day gifts of the Spirit, I will offer this last clincher, this piece of scripture. It is Romans 11:29:

[29] For the gifts and calling of God are without repentance.

A more modern translation would be they are irrevocable. Enough said, I believe.

Now concerning the gifts, there is one gift in particular, which Paul admonishes us to desire. It is the most single gift seen used by God's prophets, He even uses the word *covet* and explains why when he says in 1 Corinthians 14:1-5:

[1] Follow after charity, and desire spiritual gifts, but rather that ye may prophesy.

[2] For he that speaketh in an unknown tongue speaketh not unto men, but unto God: for no man understandeth him; howbeit in the spirit he speaketh mysteries.

[3] But he that prophesieth speaketh unto men to edification, and exhortation, and comfort.

[4] He that speaketh in an unknown tongue edifieth himself; but he that prophesieth edifieth the church.

[5] I would that ye all spake with tongues, but rather that ye prophesied: for greater is he that prophesieth than he that speaketh with tongues, except he interpret, that the church may receive edifying.

Here, the word *edify* means "to enlighten or educate." Such is necessary when the church or Christians are confronted with new circumstances or hardships, but today, prophets and prophecy themselves have been pretty much silenced. Why?

It is easily understandable why concerning a world where powers are so entangled with worldly institutions. Such powers can be both secular and religious as seen in ancient Israel and Judah, for the ones telling the prophets to silence themselves were the evil kings, priests, and false prophets who were doing the will of their father, Satan. In America, there is a separation of church and state because the powers and institutions became so entangled in Europe that free worship was curtailed, so true believers came to America. Sadly, the same has, by and large, happened in America, as many churches have sold out because they fear losing the tax free benefit afforded religious organizations.

Other churches and denominations have accepted docrtrine forbidden by scripture that they may remain vogue in a world where many of scripture's conservative teachings are concerned. This is not only a shame, but a damnable practice, for as noted earlier, God is unchanging. If your pastor teaches even one thing that is at odds with scripture, and that scripture is clearly unambiguous, I advise you to find another church immediately, and tell the pastor why. He needs to at least give you a reason, for that may cause him to act otherwise.

But why would true believers (some are surely believers albeit misinformed) try to stifle the voice of those who would be prophets? They are, inadvertently, working in tandem with the other side, or

Satan, just as those crucifying Jesus did. They are the ones Jesus prayed about and forgave when he said from the cross, "Father, forgive them, for they know not what they do." They, in their ignorance, are blameless, unless they hold on to ignorance out of pride. Many would lose powerful (if only in their eyes) positions should they admit their seeing the truth, thus carry on as is.

Others will not accept these scriptural truths because it is easier to reject these truths and justify why no such manifestation of miracles are visible in their lives. If they claim to believe manifestations of the gifts are no longer possible because of a couple of scriptures taken out of context, they do not have to answer why, even to themselves, such gifts aren't visible in their lives.

If they teach this to others, others will support and reinforce this fallacy, over years, decades, and centuries, this belief can become so ingrained that those holding on to it are innocent in that they wholeheartedly hold such as truth. That is until someone breaks out the flashlight and shines it upon their error. Then there is no excuse.

The group who hald fast to what they no believe I feel for. These are those who've attended a church since childhood, and who have friends and family they love and love to associate with, yet they've realized the ere in their denominations doctrine and stay out of loyalty. Though I understand their loyalty, imagine if they left, and in doing so, those they loved came to know the truth that together they might lead a much more productive spiritual life. A life where the Holy Spirit isn't handcuffed by belief in a false doctrine.

Why, you may ask, would I wish to reveal their error and, if they see it, cause them to become culpable concerning their present belief in a falsehood where otherwise they could die in blissful, sinless ignorance?

I wish to reveal this truth because the truth always seeks the light of day. Because the gift of prophecy is necessary, or it would have never taken such a place of prominence in the unfolding of God's plan.

Under the auspice of the Holy Spirit, the gift of prophecy is an awesome thing, so much so that Paul himself admonished us to covet it. If he admonished us to covet it, it is not an unobtainable goal. No, everyone will not receive this gift, for not all are willing to make the sacrifice necessary to gain such a wonderful blessing. Many are called, but few are chosen. Out of many thousands, Jesus chose only twelve. Are you willing to step out, for the Originator is seeking those willing to do so? Tomorrow, I will discuss the power behind the gift—the Holy Spirit. It will be power packed.

THE ESSENCE OF POWER

Have you ever heard the saying "money is the root of all evil"? I have heard that phrase being misquoted while attributed to scripture on numerous occasions. The reason I write this is to emphasize the need to not just blindly accept what someone tells you (or what I tell you) without seeing if it is accurate. Everyone's assertions should be backed by scripture or observable physical evidence. The actual quote is "Love of money is the root of all evil" (1 Timothy 6:10).

Money, just like a statuesque work of art, isn't evil, although many would say you are an idol worshiper if you own a statue. Some people want to condemn you to hell for a thousand unimportant reasons and will twist scripture to do so. Now if you love that statue and worship it, as many do where money is concerned, it is a completely different story. But why is love of money the root of all evil?

The answer is simple. Money gives the possessor the one thing almost everyone craves as if it were a necessity akin to food and shelter. Money conveys power to whoever accumulates a great amount of it. When my wife and I graduated from college, the economy was so depressed (although it was just a recession) we had to live in public housing for a short time, for jobs were hard to find. The duplex in which we lived was a dilapidated, roach-infested nightmare; and I, having just graduated from America's oldest public university, never dreamed I'd experience such. Yet there I was, and my foolish pride was ripped to shreds.

But there I learned perhaps the greatest lesson of my life. Those living there, no matter how down-and-out, were, in many ways, no different from I. Some, because of bad personal choices and others due to factors beyond their control, were there to teach me something, and it was up to me to learn this difficult lesson. If the same nightmare seems to be repeating in your life, you are just not listening to the teacher, so you aren't able to pass the test; therefore, you must repeat it.

Some were on their way up, while others were in an ever-accelerating free fall, aware of it yet with their foot pressing the accelerator with all their might. If you feel as if you are driving off a cliff, pull over and take your foot off the pedal of pride fueled by the lust for power. Power is refined usually from the vast, renewable, almost-endless supply of money. It isn't money but what money can buy (power) that drives almost all people.

This need to quell the desire for more money becomes an insatiably addictive fiend that's overwhelming. It is a cow always grazing in search of greener pastures as those fearing withdrawal seek to feed and fatten the golden bull they've come to worship.

This desire for power itself is rooted in pride. This makes sense when we consider what got us in the mess in the first place. Lucifer, upon learning of the Originator's plan for man, got his feelings hurt, became sullen and angry, stewed on it, formed a plan, and ultimately, acted on it. Until the moment he acted on it, he had done nothing wrong, but the moment he acted, rebellion on a scale we can't imagine took place. And it all had to do with pride. Unless you are the Supreme Being, it doesn't matter how much pride or power you have. Your will, when the two wills come into conflict, is always secondary. The only way to change that is to depose any power above you except God.

Stripping it down as bare as possible, it comes down to me, me, me. This attitude is so apparent today in the eyes and voices of politicians, famous entertainers, intellectuals, religious leaders, business leaders, bureaucrats, and a thousand different talking heads of myriad colors.

Businesses fail, marriages fail, countries go to war, people die, and the well-being of even our planet is now threatened because of our insatiable desire for money, which garners power, which is necessary to ensure the unsaved possessor's pride doesn't diminish. Pride and power are inextricably linked. Today, I will deal with the answer to all of today's dilemmas.

If you want true power, you *must* submit to the One True Power, or all is in vain. Why would anyone want to follow the created (including self) rather than the Creator from whom all power flows? But to plug into the original and ultimate power source, we must know where to look, and it certainly isn't in an oil reserve in some distant desert or hidden deep beneath the ocean floor. Scripture tells us where to look in our search for the immeasurable power we all were created and destined to have before man's fall from grace. Understanding scripture you will realize this power.

The power we were destined to have was the ability enjoyed by Old and New Testament prophets. It was, and is even now for the redeemed, the assurance that anything God asks us to do is back by God's omnipotent power.

You think if there was anyone in the world who wouldn't need this ultimate power source, it would be none other than God himself in the form of Jesus. Yet we see when John the Baptist baptized Jesus, the Holy Spirit fully manifested itself in the form of a dove.

Isn't it amazing the ultimate power would show itself in a form associated with peace? This wasn't by accident either, for God deals with us in ways we can understand, and he is, above all, a being of peace otherwise our obliteration wouldn't be a possibility but a reality. He could, should he desire, just wipe the slate clean and begin again, problem solved, end of story. Start over.

It is a good thing I am not the Supreme Being, for on a bad day, you would all be in trouble. I am fallible as was Lucifer, which is why his desire was anathema in the eyes of God. Fallibility leads to corruption, which leads to dissent, which leads to destruction, which leads to obliteration.

Had Lucifer won, all that is now would in time cease to exist, or at the very least, reality would change constantly. A being that has already proven itself incapable of remaining unchanged could not be trusted, as Satan has already proven he isn't unchanging. He could change everything on a whim if he became the Almighty. Lucifer once pledged allegiance to his creator. When his mind changed, his allegiance changed. If this is the reality you wish, this is what you will get for all eternity. It will be hell.

That happening, however, we do not have to worry about, for such is the power of the Creator. God, using a very small minority of mankind, has been able to frustrate Satan. Satan has pretty much the world (he won it from Adam, even saying it was his when he tempted Jesus) and all its institutions at his disposal.

Still, God's will reigns supreme, and God has been able to carry his will out even though he, through cryptic prophecy, has shown his hand before the cards were even dealt. God cannot be accused of playing unfairly. When he finally announces judgment, no one, including Satan, will be able to cry foul, for the scales will be perfectly balanced according to God's nature.

But why does God wish us to be endowed with such great power? Is it to allow us to do as our human nature would have us do, to strut our stuff? God, like any good parent, isn't going to give us anything that causes our own harm; even though we ask. So why such a gift?

The answer is found in 1 Corinthians 2:4-5:

[4] My message and my preaching were not with wise and persuasive words, but with a demonstration of the Spirit's power,

[5] so that your faith might not rest on men's wisdom, but on God's power.

The primary reason believers are entrusted with such a great power is so we will not be deceived by charlatans using wise and persuasive words as they attempt to sell snake oil.

If Jesus, were he a charlatan, could have been the best, for according to scripture, he was quite the orator. This is made clear in John 7:45-46:

[45] Then came the officers to the chief priests and Pharisees; and they said unto them, Why have ye not brought him?

[46] The officers answered, Never man spake like this man.

These officers were temple guards who the Pharisees sent with the explicit order to arrest Jesus. But something amazing happened to these hardened guards. They, after hearing someone speak as no one had ever spoken before, disobeyed a direct order and yet still reported back to the Pharisees issuing this order.

Throngs surrounded Jesus wherever he went and listened to his every word. If anyone could have pulled the proverbial wool over anyone's eyes, it would have been Jesus. Still, the very man called the Word admonished men not to go solely by what he said.

This is made clear in scripture. Jesus says in John 10:38,

[38] But if I do, though ye believe not me, believe the works: that ye may know, and believe, that the Father is in me, and I in him.

Again, he says it in John 14:11:

[11] Believe me that I [am] in the Father, and the Father is in me: or else believe me for the very works' sake.

The apostles also confirmed the purpose of visible miracles in several verses scattered throughout the New Testament.

One example is found in John 20:30-31:

[30] And many other signs truly did Jesus in the presence of His disciples, which are not written in this book;

[31] but these are written, that ye might believe that Jesus is the Christ, the Son of God; and that believing ye might have life through His name.

The apostles also had signs and miracles following them as evidence of God's calling and revelation through them. This is found in 2 Corinthians 12:12:

[12] Truly the signs of an apostle were wrought among you in all patience, in signs, and wonders, and mighty deeds.

Reading the verses mentioned, and others, it becomes abundantly clear what the purpose of the gifts of the Spirit is. It is to separate the real thing from that which is counterfeit. Think about it. If someone tells you God gave them a message concerning you, you would, even though it is something you dearly want to hear, harbor some doubt. I mean, it isn't every day someone comes to you with a message from God, and no matter how desperate you may be, such a message is all but unfathomable. Many in the world are desperate to hear the true message but, instead, are opting for anything that makes any kind of sense.

But if you actually see someone doing miracles or there is irrefutable evidence of miracles in someone's life, you listen when they talk, plain and simple. Nobody should be believed based only on their word. If you are the real thing, then let me see in your life what Jesus said would be present in the lives of all believers. Let me see signs as evidence in accordance with scripture. The signs need not be spectacular. Teaching is a sign, but most of the miracles worked by teachers are unobserved.

Spectacular signs and miracles are not mainly for Christians. Believers know scripture to be true; therefore, they can depend on the truth as revealed by scripture. But God knows unbelievers often need more to unseat deep-seated, honestly held beliefs and convictions. And things may arise that are not covered by scripture, so signs are then a necessity. They may also be needed when one sincerely believes a false doctrine to be true, for signs and miracles do grab one's attention.

Even for those who believe, and whose doctrine is sound, signs and miracles are vital in that they instruct and edify the Body of Christ, which is the church, which is his bride, which gives birth to the children of God. No father is going to leave his children to wander in the wilderness alone. He gives us His Spirit with power as evidenced by signs and miracles.

Since Adam and Eve, God has revealed prophecy and performed miracles. He did through the patriarchs, the prophets and Judges, Jesus, the apostles, and the early church. Even post early-Church history is replete with the observation of miracles when necessary.

God isn't asleep at the steering wheel. This is the way it was and is meant to be, for God is unchanging, and scripture is absolutely clear the gifts would be manifested in the Body of Christ to the edification of his Body until that which is perfect is come (Jesus), and our ability to possess perfect knowledge is given and realized according to scripture.

This perfect knowledge isn't, nor can it be entrusted to yet-perfect children as seen when Adam and Eve were forbidden to eat from the tree of life. Obviously, such knowledge is far beyond our scope and, it seems, would give the possessor the ability to figure out how to prolong life forever. Perhaps there is a reason the human brain is used at only a 10 percent capacity.

Tomorrow, we will continue discussing the Holy Spirit and his relationship with true believers and how only in submission are we able to receive and use this awesome power. I assure you, you will hear a few things you have never heard before.

TO TALK A GOOD TALK OR WALK A GOOD WALK

Sorry, but today, I am mentally beat, physically worn down, and just plain tired, so I will not be doing any research (not unless something really moves me) or write on what I'd planned. However, after reading yesterday's scripture where Jesus admonished the throngs following him to believe because as he said in John 10:38:

38. But if I do, though ye believe not me, believe the works: that ye may know, and believe, that the Father is in me, and I in him.

Again, he says it in John 14:11:

11. Believe me that I am in the Father, and the Father is in me: or else believe me for the very works' (miracles) sake.

If I give you all this fancy talk about what our purpose is—God's plan for us and the power behind the means to accomplish his will through committed, dedicated, unselfish, faith-filled, Spirit-powered believers—yet you see no evidence confirming what I am saying, then what I am saying is worse than drivel.

If I tell you I believe God will provide the sold-out believer with whatever is necessary, yet I live in poverty (I have, but he brought me out, and no, all paupers aren't going to hell, remember Lazarus in Luke 16:19-31?), you should run.

However, if quite the opposite is true and there is numerous verifiable and visible evidence that I speak the truth, draw whatever conclusion you would like, but do not run—at least consider the possibility I speak the truth. It is now an hour past noon here in Amsterdam, and I had planned a whole different subject to discuss, but I believe the life of every true believer is as described (or should be) in John 3:8:

[8] The wind bloweth where it listeth, and thou hearest the sound thereof, but canst not tell whence it cometh, and whither it goeth: so is every one that is born of the Spirit.

We should all be willing to do as we are moved by the Spirit without regard to whether we understand what is going on. If you are worried about what is happening, or going to happen, your focus is off God's will and diminishes. His ability to work in and through you becomes greatly diminished, and it gives root to doubt.

When I moved to Amsterdam last September, I had no idea what his plan was (now I do), for I would never have had the courage or isolation giving time to write this. We have a three-year contract here, but I know we will be moving back shortly (we have no job over there yet), for he wants me back home to do I know not what (though I believe it involves this).

Watch and see if I move and whether or not my family and I land on our feet without being harmed. I am telling you ahead of it happening what to watch for. I am willing to make a fool out of myself to prove my point. Watch it come to fruition. He has not failed me yet.

I decided to write this after commenting on someone's comment concerning a blog I posted yesterday on MySpace. It will be the contents of the next paragraph:

God always welcomes you back, Bonnie. Concerning hell, I once fasted and prayed for a greater appreciation and burden for the unsaved. Being a newly diagnosed diabetic (early twenties), I had no idea of the danger. There was a revival that week, and I had started going to a charismatic-type church. I began fasting on Sunday, and by Wednesday, I was miserably thirsty, so I began drinking water (probably saved my life), but wouldn't eat.

Friday before dawn, I thought I received a message from God saying something great was going to happen. I went to church that night all excited but only left disappointed and feeling sick in my stomach. I soon began throwing up and ended up in the hospital where I went into a four-day coma. I can assure you hell is real, but for some (God may have spared me the pain) it isn't a constant burning (the rich man in the Lazarus story was thirsty but mention no flame's torture). Still, with the constant violence eclipsing anything we can imagine and the overwhelming thirst, you do not want to experience such. The thought it was eternal was also overwhelming.

When I awoke from the coma, I was terrified and asked my pastor to pray for me. That night, I dreamed I was in the most beautiful place I could have imagined. There I heard a voice telling me, "Whenever you have a need, whatever that need, you shall receive what you need as you need it."

The next morning, I received a phone call from the billing office asking if I had insurance. I had neither insurance nor job but did have a wife and two young children.

The bill was $5,000, which in the mid-eighties was a staggering amount for an uninsured unemployed father and husband. I remembered what the voice had promised but still became angry, for I had just awaken from a four-day terror.

Two hours later, I received another phone call from the billing office telling me the bill had been paid. I will never know who paid it, but scripture tells us he will care for the believer. God was, in having the bill paid, proving himself. Jesus once told the throngs, "If you don't believe what I say (his Word), believe the signs and miracles."

Since that day, my life has been replete with such examples. After slipping into two more diabetic comas, my four-year college tuition, books, room and board, etc. were paid for. When Katrina destroyed my two-story house (remember I was once in poverty, even homeless once), I rebuilt a three-story, steel-framed house where it had stood, although two of my nearest neighbors had to move for lack of funds.

Everything I say can be backed up. Photos of my new home are on my Facebook page (I only lived in it four months before, reluctantly but obediently I came here). Nothing is set, but I know in my heart (some would call that prophecy, lol) we will be back in less than three months. You will see that if you sell out to God, he will *not* sell you out, and he has the means. Oh, and I have some nice shots of Amsterdam for proof also. Sorry for the rant, Sam DeLoach.

I never meant to put this in this series of writings, but it seemed like the right thing to do. Still, I do so with caution, for it isn't about me. Do not follow my example but Christ's. I am merely trying (emphasis on *trying*) to be a finger pointing in the right direction.

Addendum: I am entering this in September of 2024 to tell you how things worked out concerning my prophesying the move from Amsterdam. We moved within two months and my wife found job as a controller paying a wee bit less. You may think that if God was so magnificent and all powerful, why would he not insure her pay at least stay the same. God knew what he is doing, and she is now a CFO without ever getting a master's degree or a CPA, which is almost unheard of.

There are many other examples I can give, which can be verify, so when I say I am not just talking a good spiel, check it out with an open mind, and then if you'd like, just chalk all it up to luck. But if you do that, let me ask you a question. Have you ever even considered visiting or calling a fortune-teller? If you say yes but also say you do not know me, did you know them? It never ceases to amaze me the things we choose to believe and the things we choose not to believe.

Do you feel there should be, according to scriptural teachings, much more *evidence* of physical manifestations of the power Jesus spoke of and that such should be visible in today's churches? Do you feel the churches are full of honest, true believers awaiting the truth, which will unshackle them from the chains of doubt and disbelief concerning God's true purpose and the power, signs and miracles enabling them to tell the world what it is? Are you willing to fly?

Enough about me. From now on, I plan to hold the discussion of self to a bare minimum, for it isn't at all about me, and if I fall into that deep pit, how can I help anyone out of whatever pit (spiritual, physical, or financial, etc.) they may be in? Tomorrow, we get better acquainted with the grand Spirit of Power. 9/23/24

WHAT'S LOVE GOT TO DO WITH IT?

Perhaps I should cease stating with such certainty what tomorrow's lesson is going to be, for though I might have an idea, even as I sit to write, I am not exactly sure what is about to unfold. Today, I would like to reveal much about the person of the Holy Spirit. First, let's touch on the Godhead. Most Christians believe in a triune (three persons in one being) Godhead. There are Christians, however, who do not believe in a triune god; and I, for one, will not condemn them to hell or rant about their being wrong.

I ask they pray for me to find the truth, and I will do the same for them and hope we all keep an open mind, for a closed hand (mind) can grasp nothing. If we all did this, there would be much less acrimony between different faiths; and I believe most would eventually realize the truth, for the truth would then be free to reveal itself in signs and miracles no one could deny.

I remember listening to a sermon one night many years ago. I believe the scripture used that night concerned Joseph's ability to dream and interpret dreams, but I am not certain. I do remember the preacher telling the congregation of another preacher with this same ability. This pastor lost his wallet and, after praying about it, went to sleep that night. That night, he had a dream. In the dream, he found his wallet. The next morning, he went to the location where he dreamed he found it, and it was right there. Some in the congregation seemed amazed at this recounting. I wasn't amazed but assured or, I should say, reassured.

When I was five, I dreamed I found a black plastic spider about the size of a child's hand. In this dream, I found it buried underneath some leaves, which were placed around an azalea to protect the roots. The dream seemed so real.

A few days later, my mom came from Savannah (we lived on a farm thirty miles from town) with a plastic spider just like the one in my dream; only this one had a pencil sharpener inside of it. The next day, I took it to school and placed it in my desk. I left it in my desk when I went out to recess.

When I came back inside from recess, I reached into my desk to withdraw my pencil sharpener. It wasn't there. As I rifled through the desk in desperation, Ms. Knight asked, "What are you doing, Sammy?"

As she asked the question, I remembered my dream. I quickly asked if I could go outside for a minute, for I knew where my sharpener was. She complied. I went out and looked beneath an azalea bush planted beside the school and began searching through the leaves. As I dug through the leaves, it was as if I were reliving the dream. Still, I was shocked when, lo and behold, it was lying in the same position it was when I found it in the dream. That string of events has always stood out in my mind.

Throughout my life, such has happened over and over. I know I said yesterday I wouldn't say much more about me, but you will see where I am going, for I do have a point greater than self.

I never had such a vivid dream involving something, which would later be revealed, until I was seventeen. Only this time, there would be years, not days, between the initial dream and my understanding it. It involved the Holy Spirit.

In my dream, God was talking to me (pretty grandiose dream, huh?). I believe some believers, as children of the Originator of all life, should be able to have such dreams, for scripture says God is no respecter of persons. He does, however, respect faith.

When I woke up from sleeping, the dream seemed so real that I felt God was actually trying to explain some great mystery. But I was completely unable to grasp it until earlier this year, which is some thirty-five years later. And Psalms repeats, "Wait upon the Lord" over and over for a purpose.

In the dream, I saw God telling me his Holy Spirit was the blood that bound us together in much the same manner my blood binds me and my father. It sounded good, but I missed it completely.

Earlier, I told you I came to Amsterdam for the purpose of beginning this series of blogs. To do so, I needed to find a book containing apocryphal scripture. Most will say apocryphal scripture has been disavowed by church orthodoxy. I even accept that some (much or most in some books) of it is in error. Some books are almost completely in error. But what I read in the Gospel of Philip opened my eyes, and I understood suddenly a mystery hidden for years.

I myself find much of this particular gospel beyond comprehension because of its rambling form. There are no chapters or verses, just a random amalgamation of thoughts, or so it seems. However, three successive sentences flew from the pages as I skimmed them with little concentration on what I was reading. One of the sentences could have been lifted directly from John 6:53, and it was the first of the series of sentences.

The series of sentence reads as such: "Because of this he said, 'He who shall not eat my flesh and drink my blood has not life in him.' [same as John 6:53]. What is it? His flesh is the word, and his blood is the Holy Spirit. He who has received these has food and he has drink and clothing." That in brackets in this paragraph is my interjection.

When first reading this, I freaked, for here in a long-banished forgotten scripture found buried in a cave near Nag Hammadi in 1945, I was hearing what I had heard thirty-five years earlier, and the light switch flipped on, and the current flowed.

So what does this mean, and what is the Holy Spirit's role in the life of a believer? What I am about to reveal blew my mind.

Before Christ's coming, Israel was often referred to as an adulterous wife, with God being the husband. Since Christ's began his ministry, and announced the kingdom of heaven was at hand in Mathew 3:2, the church has been, and is, referred to as the bride of Christ.

What do brides and wives do? Well, they do many things, but the most important thing any of us do here on earth, besides serving God, is ensure the continuation of the species by the birthing process. Wives give birth in families as sanctioned by God in marriage. This is what he intended with Adam and Eve and, through them and their offspring, was how he planned to bring his family into being. Through humanity, God desired to birth a family of triune beings.

The Church is not a building at all; it is the worldwide body of believers who, by the presentation of the truth as witnessed in their lives and by their lifestyles, brings others into the fold. Also, the resulting signs and miracles that should follow all believers draw nonbelievers to Christ as planned by God. 9/24/24

When anyone not believing in God's plan of salvation crosses the threshold and becomes a true believer, an unseen transformation occurs, which we are simply unable to fully comprehend, much less appreciate. Spiritually speaking, there is more difference between a saved person and an unsaved person than there is between a human and a rock. One is living. The other has known life. That might sound arrogant or cruel, but it is scripturally sound. Let's look at a couple of scriptures confirming my assertions.

The first is John 6:53:

[53] Then Jesus said unto them, Verily, verily, I say unto you, Except ye eat the flesh of the Son of man, and drink his blood, ye have no life in you.

Remember the scripture from the Gospel of Philip I wrote of earlier being the same as the one just written?

Again, Jesus says in Luke 9:59-60,

[59] And he said unto another, Follow me. But he said, Lord, suffer me first to go and bury my father.

[60] *Jesus* said unto him, Let the dead bury their dead: but go thou and preach the kingdom of God.

Although this sounds cruel, Jesus was making an important point. The unsaved are, spiritually speaking, dead.

Not only are they dead in the eyes of God, they are also dead in the eyes of all spiritual beings. I know this may sound amazing but listen to what happened in Acts when the unsaved tried to exercise a demon-possessed man using the name of Jesus as the apostles had done and were doing.

This is shown in Acts 19:13-16:

[13]—Then certain of the vagabond Jews, exorcists, took upon them to call over them which had evil spirits (using) the name of the Lord Jesus, saying, We adjure you by Jesus whom

Paul preacheth.

[14]—And there were seven sons of one Sceva, a Jew, and chief of the priests, which did so.

[15]—And the evil spirit answered and said, Jesus I know, and Paul I know; but who are ye?

[16]—And the man in whom the evil spirit was leaped on them, and overcame them, and prevailed against them, so that they fled out of that house naked and wounded.

You want power? It doesn't come from the dark side, and true power isn't wielded by nonbelievers, no matter how it appears to the world around us.

The reason unbelievers are referred to as being dead is they, in the spiritual realm, are. Such has been the case since the moment Adam and Eve bit the apple (remember it is a metaphor, and the Bible never describes the fruit as being an apple).

But the moment you come to realize and accept the truth in repentance, a wonderful transformation takes place, and your reality is forever changed.

This is made clear in 1 Peter 1:23:

Being born again, not of corruptible seed, but of incorruptible, by the word of God, which liveth and abideth for ever.

The moment we pass over the threshold from spiritual death into eternal life, an incorruptible seed is planted in us, but that is only in accordance to God's original plan for Adam.

God is the master of metaphor. Over and over, he uses metaphor to reveal his plan. Circumcision was a metaphor (a painful one at that) for the conversion of the heart. Saul's rejection by God and subsequent replacement by David as the king of the Jewish nation is a metaphor in which Saul is the Jewish people and David is the Church or Bride of Christ.

Over and over, scripture uses metaphor to shed light on what is so hard to understand. And what better metaphor is there for God's plan for mankind than the womb? In the womb, we have a corruptible seed planted and nurtured until it is able to, after birth, live as an individual fleshly human.

This fleshly body is meant for but one purpose, just as the womb is—to give birth. Only now the incorruptible is, like a fetus, maturing until it is ready to be born, which happens when we the seed, God's word is planted in it by hearing or reading scripture. Once the seed is accepted, and takes root upon accepting Jesus as Lord and Savior, a marvel occurs, and a spiritual birth happens when the Holy Spirit enters us. Then and only then are we the full-fledged triune beings God wanted all along. When I realized this recently, it made so much sense and seemed so simple I wonder why I'd never seen it. But it gets even better.

Just as a fetus is nurtured by the blood of his or her mother while in the womb, we who believe are nurtured by the Spirit, which is the Trinity's blood, until we are again birthed in dying, wherein we don our new, incorruptible bodies, and are bothered by temptation never again.

Even then, we retain the spiritual blood just as we have and keep the blood of our parents (we will still possess our bodies. Now think of a fetus in the womb; without nourishment from its mother it wouldn't stand a chance. The same is so for spiritual fetuses, which is the incorruptible seed Peter writes of. We need this blood, for it nurtures and sustains us. But it does more than that—much more.

His Spirit, which he gives to each believer, is that which unites us (believers) all and brings us into God's family, just like blood is the substance uniting families, peoples, and indeed, all humanity. It, like faith, is the evidence of things yet seen, substance of things hoped for. It, like blood, is the common denominator for the great family of triune beings God is now gathering during this period in creation. Time, I believe, is quickly running out (if you believe anything I say, believe this).

There is another reason Jesus had to die besides his paying the price for all our sins. Before Jesus's death, resurrection, and ascension, the Holy Ghost was not free to come in its fullness. There are a couple of reasons why this is so.

Both have to do with the balancing of the scales. In dying, Jesus balanced the scales of sin sent out of kilter when Satan had an innocent man wrongly put to death, giving Jesus the right to undo what Adam had done in his original act of disobedience as I explained before. This gave Jesus the right to claim the sins of all who would accept his sacrifice through wrongful death and allowed him to bear the sins of those who would come to believe.

But this also disallowed the following argument. Satan could not say a man would never be willing to shed his blood for God as God wanted and needed to do for humanity. Whereas Abraham had already proven a man was willing to shed his child's innocent blood in obedience to God, Jesus actually did it. In this act, Jesus represents Isaac, and the Father represents Abraham. God so loves metaphor.

In giving his Spirit (blood) to create the family he so desired, the Originator was willing to watch his son suffer a horrible death. Jesus, a willingly innocent victim, silenced any argument Satan had on both accounts. In shedding his physical blood in the form of man on God's behalf, it allowed God to shed his spiritual blood (the Holy Spirit) on man's behalf.

So the blood uniting us with the Godhead is the Holy Spirit. It is what we all, the three persons in the Godhead and all believers, share in common. It is what unites us and brings us into the great family of like, triune beings, which was the Creator's purpose the moment he conceived his great plan for a material universe.

How the universe got here is of no consequence in the grand scheme of things. That we are here and that God, in this realm, has made a way whereby we can become part of his family is most amazing. It is the fulfillment of the plan of "he that openeth, and no man shutteth; and shutteth, and no man openeth;" (Revelation 3:7). It was destined to happen by he who destines all.

Now that we understand the Holy Spirit and its purpose a bit better, we shall move on.

ONE DAY AT A TIME

Nobody likes being used. Have you ever heard anyone say, "She (or he) just used me" or "It wasn't really me he wanted, it was..." or "I feel so used"? Being used is not fun. Usually, the only one gaining any benefits is the user, not the usee. And the world is full of users, merciless users. Users are about only one thing—self. Such is the basic nature of humans, for they are the seed of the ultimate user, Satan.

But there is one example where the long-term user-usee relationship is turned on its head. In this relationship, the more you allow yourself to be used, the greater the benefits. Such sounds strange, doesn't it? As far as this world is concerned, it is contrary to everything we've ever known or observed. Yet it is the only way we are able to reach anything anywhere near our full potential and realize a sense of complete, unadulterated confidence otherwise impossible to fathom. And it isn't prideful self-confidence extolled by the world, it is selfless confidence.

If I was looking for answers in a troubled world (you can't say ours isn't) and someone promised me I could, without forking over money (run if I ask for money), unlock an endless treasure trove enabling me to do the unimaginable, I would listen. If (again, involving no money) someone asked me to try something for just a couple of weeks to see if I realized a difference in my life able to unlock this trove, I'd be inclined to think about it and, at least, consider it.

What I am speaking about has never been attained by any system, government, or philosophy implemented, or even conceived of here on earth during the thousands of years of civilized man. Throughout the many centuries, numerous great and powerful civilizations have risen and fallen, usually rotting from within as their society becomes self-consumed. Babylon, Persia, Greece, Rome, Spain, England, the Incan Empire, the Mayan Empire, China, the Khmer Rouge, and countless unknown empires have all risen to great power only to watch their civilizations crumble. Even now, America seems to be spiraling down the drain due to excess and self-adulation.

But it doesn't have to be that way where you are concerned, for even as the whole world is spiraling down, you can soar. Imagine if in your hand you hold a few old coins, which, if you are willing to release, would enable you to reach into the storehouse whenever you need. You only need to open your fist and release what you've held for so long. If you are looking for more, release what you cling to.

With the Supreme User, what we perceive the moral decay as reality seems convoluted, and may wish God to step in and take authoritarian control. But doing such is against God's, the giver of free will, nature. He forces nothing. If he did, all things would be his way right now, and we would have no free will and no choice. He, the puppet maker, could be the puppet master, but that isn't his way.

Our Creator will only use you as much as you allow him to. But if you allow him to, he will use you in ways you cannot begin to imagine, let alone comprehend. What makes him different from all the other users? First, he needs nothing whatsoever since all that exists comes from him.

Second, it is his nature to do good. And third, he desires you to help spread his nature to all that is. In doing so, you will become part of the Being that is good. There is only one source of good or goodness. This is made clear in Luke 18:19:

[19] And *Jesus* said unto him, Why callest thou me good? none is good, save one, that is, God (Mark 10:18).

In case some think this scripture indicates Jesus is not part of the Godhead, I recommend you looking to see what other scripture says, for in this verse, Jesus didn't say he wasn't god or that he wasn't good. When anyone claims the Bible says something, cross-reference it to see if it meshes with other scripture, for scripture is so often taken out of context and even twisted to conform to someone's particular agenda. Also, any scripture worth cinching your belt around is usually backed by many verses supporting each other.

I will list four that should settle any argument concerning Jesus's divinity. They are as follows:

1. John 9:38: "Then he said, 'Lord, I believe!' And he worshiped Him."
2. Mark 5:6: "When he saw Jesus from afar, he ran and worshiped Him."
3. Matthew 15:25: "Then she came and worshiped Him, saying, 'Lord, help me!'"
4. Matthew 2:11: "And when they had come into the house, they saw the young Child with Mary His mother, and fell down and worshiped Him. And when they had opened their treasures, they presented gifts to Him: gold, frankincense, and myrrh."
5. Isaiah 9:6: [6] For unto us a child is born, unto us a son is given: and the government shall be upon his shoulder: and his name shall be called Wonderful, Counsellor, The mighty God, The everlasting Father, The Prince of Peace.

I consider Isaiah 9:6 to be a clincher, for not only did he prophecy The Prince of Peace's birth, he did so some seven hundred years before the birth of Christ. He also proclaimed Jesus *The mighty God*. In my mind this seals it. I had a friend I known for years, and someone had him convinced of this until I show him the above verse. If only he'd read his bible. Do you?

Now back to my point. All goodness originates and flows from one source. It is the power that created the universe and the source of the constant power throughout the universe. The law of the conservation of energy (a law of science, not a theory) states energy can't be created or destroyed, only moved from place to place. Since energy has remained constant throughout the universe since creation and can't be created or destroyed,

I argue the origination source of the material universe and its *energy* is none other than that which is good. I believe God to be pure energy, a scientific theory concerning an energy having no reaction with the four states of matter or the four sttes of energy. This sounds like the fire that Moses spoke with that was o the bush, burning, yet not consuming the bush, or the flames alighting on those at Pentecost. Again I digress.

If you desire to do good, it is absolutely necessary you be plugged into and drawing from the only and ultimate power source, since universal power is constant and singular. As a matter of fact, I find it amazing the world's foremost scientists, especially physicists, believe the big bang sprang from a single point they call the quantum singularity. If that doesn't make you think "Wow," I am puzzled. In my mind, even the most advanced scientific theory screams of a single creator. Call it what you wish; I call it God.

Now this universe isn't all there is. Paul spoke of such in 2 Corinthians 12:2-4:

[2] I knew a man in Christ above fourteen years ago, (whether in the body, I cannot tell; or whether out of the body, I cannot tell: God knoweth;) such an one caught up to the third heaven.

[3]—And I knew such a man, (whether in the body, or out of the body, I cannot tell: God knoweth;) [4]—How that he was caught up into paradise, and heard unspeakable words, which it is not lawful for a man to utter.

Many scientists now think we live in a multiverse, which is the hypothetical set of multiple possible universes (including our universe) that together comprise everything that physically exists: the entirety of space and time; all forms of matter, energy, and momentum; and the physical laws and constants. I find it strange the further science advances, the more wonderful God appears.

Addendum: I now believe some planes of existence need not be physical. Some could be made of pure energy – who knows? Heaven is filled with being that, though they are not physical, live, and are even able to take physical form. Energy (having no mass; taking up no space), can as I explained be converted into matter (photosynthesis). We see matter turning into almost pure energy in a nuclear explosion.

Reality is proving itself to be stranger than even modern man, let alone ancient man, could have dreamed. And the author of all—the entirety of space and time; all forms of matter, energy, and momentum; and the physical laws and constants—is our Creator.

Talk about power! You want power? He desires you to have it. But there is a single caveat. It is only given to the selfless, not the selfish. The more selfless you are, the more he can use you; the more he can use you, the more he gives you. God gives you nothing to hoard. In fact, God doesn't approve of hoarding whatsoever.

This is made clear in the parable where Jesus states in Luke 12:*15 -22*:

15 - And he said unto them, Take heed, and beware of covetousness: for a man's life consisteth not in the abundance of the things which he possesseth.

16 - And he spake a parable unto them, saying, The ground of a certain rich man brought forth plentifully:

17 - And he thought within himself, saying, What shall I do, because I have no room where to bestow my fruits?

18 - And he said, This will I do: I will pull down my barns, and build greater; and there will I bestow all my fruits and my goods.

19 -And I will say to my soul, Soul, thou hast much goods laid up for many years; take thine ease, eat, drink, [and] be merry.

20 - But God said unto him, [Thou] fool, this night thy soul shall be required of thee: then whose shall those things be, which thou hast provided?

21 - So [is] he that layeth up treasure for himself, and is not rich toward God.

22 - And he said unto his disciples, Therefore I say unto you, Take no thought for your life, what ye shall eat; neither for the body, what ye shall put on.

That were a few more verses than I'd planned, but these prove my point so well. Jesus isn't saying all who covet are going to die right away. We can look around and see such isn't so. He is just making the point that God hates coveting, for it works contrary to everyone's spiritual growth, not just the coveter's spiritual growth.

God gives to us so we can share with others. As God blesses us, using himself as the ultimate, inexhaustible source, he expects us to share his blessings. This we see abundantly in the life of Jesus as he ministered by feeding the hungry, healing the sick, raising the dead, and freeing the demon-possessed. In doing so, he used actions, not words, to draw the masses, going so far as to say in John 14:11,

[11] Believe me that I am in the Father, and the Father in me: or else believe me for the very works' sake.

As you allow God to use you more by divesting yourself of self, God reciprocates in measure to the level you throw off the shackles of selfishness. This goes against everything our flesh tells us, but it is fundamental to true spiritual growth and why, in today's world, we see so little evidence of the miracles Jesus spoke of.

I have read the scriptures concerning God's reciprocity based on our level of selfishness for years, but only recently have I decided to sell out, for recently, I have seen it in action in ways that have opened my eyes. It is a process that, as you grow spiritually, feeds itself.

When first reading various scriptural verses concerning the law of spiritual reciprocity, I simply didn't understand them, for they made no sense, and I could never imagine applying them to my life. For it is almost unimaginable to take no thought of what I will eat, or what I will wear, or worry about my body's health or of my life in general. I am only now beginning to grasp such, but I have seen evidence of his blessings, signs, and miracles increasing as I buy into the truth of all scripture, including this.

This is reiterated in Matthew 6:25:

[25] Therefore I say unto you, Take no thought for your life, what ye shall eat, or what ye shall drink; nor yet for your body, what ye shall put on. Is not the life more than meat, and the body than raiment?

Doing the above comes with a conditional promise Jesus gives in Matthew 6:33-34:

[33] But seek ye first the kingdom of God, and his righteousness; and all these things shall be added unto you.

[34] Take therefore no thought for the morrow: for the morrow shall take thought for the things of itself. Sufficient unto the day is the evil thereof.

There is no metaphor in these two verses. They are straightforward and plain. Although such a lifestyle is very hard to accept literally, it is even more difficult to live, for we must absolutely let go of self and self-control. This is anathema to human nature.

Why would God want it this way? Some things are so simple they are, it seems, almost beyond our grasp. If we truly do this, we are forced to depend on God's goodwill and his ability to manage our destiny better than we can.

If we are able to trust God, he proves himself to us, and he never fails. If he never fails, our faith grows as we overcome the ever-increasing obstacles Satan places in our path. We in turn become the spiritual warriors and maturing children God so desires. I am afraid the afterlife will be full of God's progeny who are far less mature than he would have desired. They will be the ones with few crowns to throw at Jesus's feet when we are resurrected.

As we grow spiritually, the evidence of God's presence in our lives will be manifested in so many ways, one being the blessings we are to share with others. These blessings, if given to others in the spirit of selfless love, are a most powerful witness that we do, indeed, serve a God capable of doing the unimaginable—bridging the gap between God and man by making us members of his family.

The more Christlike we become, the more we allow him to infuse us with the power of his Holy Spirit, the blood binding all Christians with the Godhead and one another.

Boiling it down to its basic essence, the more we submit to the source from whom all power and goodness flows, the more selfless we become, and the more we are able to help others, which brings more into the family.

If I have two children—one who isn't so obedient and squanders what I give him on himself while the other is obedient, kind, and selfless—I know which one will receive what he (or she) needs as they need it, for I know it will be put to good use.

You want to be blessed? Sell out. Believe in all what God has said, not just what makes sense in light of what you have learned in this world.

Grab onto that ultimate power source, for it is a live wire. Grab it and run with it. Plug it into others, and shock them awake or, literally, shock them alive. Shock them with the love of the Almighty Single Singularity. Bring them into the fold and watch God reciprocate in ways you can't imagine.

WHO'S YOUR DADDY?

With yesterday having been Father's Day, I think today's discussion is quite apropos. I awoke this morning with no idea what I was going to write, and even as I write, I do so not knowing exactly where it will go or the scripture I'll use to back my assertions. I am trying to set an example, showing that if you take no thought of tomorrow, things can and will work out if you are working in tandem with the Originator (God). This is in accordance with what I said yesterday.

There are few blessings in life that greater than having a good, caring father. A good mother is one of the few that can equal it. Anyone having one or the other, and especially those having both, can consider themselves very fortunate.

The orphanages, juvenile detention centers, prisons, cathouses, substance-abuse treatment centers, and myriad other places most people do not want to end up would not be filled with the many people contained therein had they had a parent or parents. Many living in such places, had they been afforded a good role model, most likely would be living a completely different lifestyle.

This is not to say all wayward children have awful parents. Remember the parable concerning the prodigal son? Free will, unfortunately, sometimes eclipses good parenting. Still, the value of a good parent can't be overemphasized, for the prodigal son did return and what seemed a total eclipse ended up only a partial eclipse.

The metaphor where we are described as the seed of our ancestors is beautiful, for the father's seed (sperm) is planted in the earth (womb), where it germinates until it sprouts through the soil (comes from the womb in the birthing process).

Then it is a full-fledged individual organism whose primary purpose is to procreate and produce more like seed in kind—more corn, more peas, dogs, humans, etc. Corn never produces wheat, wheat never produces beans, frogs never reproduce puppies, and so on. There are many plants that produce seed useful to humanity, and there many producing seed that is a bane to humanity.

I grew up on a farm and remember pulling weeds from the crops in order to ensure the necessary nutrients went to the crops, not the weeds. But you had to do it before the weeds grew too big, or weed pulling would actually harm the crops by displacing too much soil when you ripped the weeds from the ground. It was best to deal with the weeds when they were young.

Humans are unlike any other creature in existence, for a tremendous gift has been bestowed upon us—the gift of free will. No other creature, all lacking free will, falls into mankind's good-seed or bad-seed category, for they have no choice what nature they will nurture. They are what they are, period. A lion eats meat, yet its violence is natural and acceptable with no thought of malice. It is culpable of nothing.

Humanity is the culmination of the Originator's grand creation process whereby he, for the first time ever, would create a family of like triune beings—the only triune beings besides himself in existence. This was his plan, and it was proceeding swimmingly until treachery unfolded.

For my proposed contention, I use the supposition there is a supreme being called God, for this is what I believe with all my heart. And by the very nature of calling him a supreme being, there can be only one else God wouldn't be supreme.

Still, it is merely a supposition for most, for in their minds only that felt, seen, heard, smelled, or tasted crosses the threshold going from supposition to certainty. And as far as certainty or supposition is concerned, those espousing the big bang theory must admit all theories are, according to science, nothing but strong suppositions until proven conclusively. And feel free to decide whether you believe in the six-day creation or the big bang, for I do not think it really matters in the Originator's eyes. Follow your heart and conscience, for that is what he judges.

A family of triune beings was the original intent of the Originator in creating the universe, and humanity is the realization of this intent. The treachery mentioned above, as I explained in a previous post, was Lucifer's rebellion caused by pride and jealousy.

Adam, the first being with the ability to reason sufficiently enough to garner the gift of free will, along with Eve, fell under Lucifer's (now called Satan) influence and disobeyed the Originator, their Creator. Because of this, their very nature changed, and they fell from grace, stalling but never changing God's original plan, for he is unchanging and his will incontrovertible.

The human body (because we could reason and were given free will) was always meant to be the temple of God. Paul calls the body of believers such in 1 Corinthians 3:16:

16 - Know ye not that ye are the temple of God, and that the Spirit of God dwelleth in you?

It is the Spirit, which we all share with other Christians, and with the Godhead that sets us apart. The Spirit is that which unites us as family. This, in the same manner our blood unites us with our immediate family and then, by extension, the entire human family, the Holy Spirit does for the family of God. This is why He fills each of us with His Holy Spirit. Though I understand and fully believe this, it is still difficult to wrap my mind around.

God's children are birthed by the Bride of Christ (the church), and by this process, the Body of Christ is created. Yes, the bride and children are of the same family, and both belong to Jesus by virtue of his ultimate sacrifice wherein he spared nothing on our behalf.

When Adam and Eve fell, God's Holy Spirit departed from their bodies in accordance to prophecy as told in Genesis: "The day ye eat of the fruit of good and evil, you will die" (paraphrased). Before the proverbial bite of the apple, Adam and Eve were of the Children of God (still needing instruction) and contained his Holy Spirit. They were given dominion over the earth. After they sinned, they became the seed of Satan, and Satan gained dominion over the earth as revealed when Satan tempted Jesus.

We see this in Matthew 4:8-9:

[8] Again, the devil taketh him up into an exceeding high mountain, and sheweth him all the kingdoms of the world, and the glory of them;

[9] And saith unto him, All these things will I give thee, if thou wilt fall down and worship me.

When the serpent (a metaphor for Satan, not a real snake) was cursed in Genesis 3:15 ("And I will put enmity between thee and the woman, and between thy seed and her seed; it shall bruise thy head, and thou shalt bruise his heel."), he gained lordship of the earth, which had been given to Adam.

What is the seed God speaks of concerning Eve? It is the word of God, both Old and New Testament scripture (both heard and read). With the planted seed, they could learn of God and come to know Christ well enough to understand the plan of salvation, and thereby become saved if they chose. One saved, they would become Children of God, and a triune being.

Through faith in the Supreme Being and his goodness, they could have occurring sin forgiven is they repented, and asked for forgiveness. Guiltfree, they come into loving obedience by believing and understanding the Creator has nothing but our goodwill at heart. When this is done by our using free will, God places his Spirit back inside the believer, and he or she is once again the temple of the Holy Spirit as was the original intention of God. If you are reading this, the only pertinent question you need ask yourself is, "Do you possess his Holy spirit?"

What or who is the seed God speaks of concerning Satan? It is all who are given the real opportunity to come to the truth yet reject the truth. Keep in mind not everyone who doesn't come to accept the truth actually reject it, for you must be exposed to something before you are able to reject it.

Now think about it. God is the creator of all things, including us. All goodness flows from him, and he intends only good for us. When trials come, it is not of God. It is of the father of the other seed (remember, seed comes from like plants or like parentage), and we obey the nature of our parents. People inherit the characteristics, traits, and temperaments of their parents to a large degree. We've all heard someone say, "You're just like you daddy" or "You look just like your mom."

I don't know about you, but I would rather have the nature of an all-powerful creator than that of a being whose claim to fame is rebellion against the one who created him, for the original act of rebellion is rooted in the sins of pride and envy. It is both pride and envy that quell the desire to reach out and receive the gift of inclusion into God's family when offered by the Creator and when the pull of conviction rakes the heart.

All problems in the world today stem from the one of the strongest desires of the father of this world. Satan's desire is the destruction of humanity. He blames his downfall on our creation. Therefore, he loathes us.

The sad thing is that Satan's seeds are completely unaware of who their father is or what his intentions are. Such is his nature. Were he to show his true hand and unveil his true intentions, all humanity would run to God. Therefore, he obfuscates and lies. Christ said that when Satan lies, he is speaking his native tongue, for he is the father of lies (John 8:44). He used a lie to deceive Eve by saying in Genesis 3:4-5,

[4] And the serpent said unto the woman, Ye shall not surely die:

[5] For God doth know that in the day ye eat thereof, then your eyes shall be opened, and ye shall be as gods, knowing good and evil.

One thing you can say about Satan: he is true to his nature. He offers over and again the very same thing that led to his downfall: power and the desire for power, ultimate power. It is this desire for power that flows from the bad-seed head that causes every problem known to mankind. The lust for power is what causes envy, covetousness (from money and property to other's spouses), thievery, murder, lies, deceit, and even war (perhaps man's greatest grab for power).

All addictions that cloud the mind or preoccupy our time to our detriment stem from a belief we will never fulfill this desire for power, so we try to stifle our selfish desire's cry for such. In doing so, we are also silencing (sometimes intentionally) the call to come to he who has our true best interest in mind—the Good Father.

He who has all power need not scheme to gain power. How many schemes arise in self-interest, stemming from the desire to attain and accumulate power? Where does such come from? Such has a father, and this trait is passed down to and through his seed. There is no need for God, or anyone doing the correct thing, to scheme.

Still, our innate desire to do that which is far less than kosher need not be. Those of the bad-father seed are not free unless they choose the plan of redemption, salvation through the cross. Once we accept God's plan of salvation, we, having God's Holy Spirit, are given immense power enabling us to reject Satan's many, and varied temptations. In choosing to sin, or not sin, the ball is now in our court, though the temptations increase as we become more faithful.

This is reality because other than his own, Satan hates freedom. Everything he offers becomes addictive, although it usually at first seems innocuous. I remember the first joint I smoked (yes, I smoked – no longer do) and the first beer I drank. Had I known, when they were first offered me, and that I would spend quite a while struggling to free myself from their grip, I would have run.

But the first high felt so liberating, as did the first drink, intoxicating (speking both literally and metaphorically). I remember laughing and no longer worrying about the little things in the beginning. Later, I forgot how to care about the important things, and I often found tears had replaced the laughter. All addicts suffer due to the seeded nature nonbelievers have from birth until they accept the freedom offered by our Creator. Today, we have workaholics, sex addicts, alcoholics, drug addicts and the list goes on.

But we do have a choice, unlike Satan, for we have the precious gift of free will, and unlike Satan, we were (through Eve) tricked into choosing sin. If you don't believe in God and don't think you will ever be able to, I don't ask you fall on your knees and ask for forgiveness (you should), for until you come to God, it isn't the nature you are seeded with.

We who are believers were once all like that, so those who have chosen to do so are no better than you. They've just been given a different nature. If you don't believe, I would like to recount this story. It is true.

There was a fourteen-year-old girl in China. Both of her parents were doctors and intellectuals who suffered greatly because of the Cultural Revolution during the late sixties and early seventies. One of her parents was sent to Mongolia, the other to Tibet for reeducation. There they worked as peasants, while my wife spent four years with one aunt and uncle, and her older sister stayed with another aunt and uncle.

One day when she was six, her parents, having become strangers, arrived and picked her sister and her up after four years and reformed the family. When she was sixteen, her father was sent to America to work at the National Institute of Health (NIH) doing cancer research (he was the number 2 cancer research scientist in China). While he was in DC, her mother committed suicide, devastating this young teenage girl.

Her father hurried home for the funeral. On the way home, he was given a Chinese bible, which he left with this girl when he returned back to Washington and the NIH. Her older sister (by two years) was attending medical college in Beijing, and she was left all alone, but for the first time, she had a Bible.

As she read it, she found it impossible to grasp the concept of God. Still, one night, she, desperate, went to her balcony and prayed this simple prayer. "I've always been told you are a crutch for the weak and an opiate of society [communist, Marxist doctrine], but if you do exist, get me to America." Imagine that leap of faith.

Six months later, she was on a plane headed for Washington DC. Her sister came two years later. They were the first family that, in totality, legally came to America after the fall of China.

A couple of years later, she attended a small college in Savannah, Georgia, because her father knew a professor and she and her sister got a special deal in that they didn't have to pay out-of-state tuition. There she met this country boy who was praying for a Christian wife, for his belief in God had been a great point of contention is his last marriage.

They met and quickly fell in love even though she thought what he believed in was folly and even though he had been praying for a Christian wife, for she was still an avowed atheist. He didn't push the point, and she made clear she couldn't and wouldn't believe in the abstract, only the tangible and the touchable.

One day, she looked at him and said, "God does not want me anyway."

To which he replied by asking, "Why?"

She looked away and declared, "Because I am empty. There is nothing inside of me—nothing!"

He cocked his head, thought for a second, and said, "If I had a great treasure, would I look for a box full of junk to place it in or a nice empty box with lots of room?" And the door was cracked.

He began to tutor her in English, and she tutored him in algebra. As she observed his life, she felt compelled to walk through the door, and he gained a Christian love who would, before long (they eloped), become his wife (as of twenty-two years right now).

Addendum: It has been thirty-eight now.

Our love has grown through the years, as has her faith, which much of the time she actually carried me. The point I am making is, if you are unsure, ask him to reveal his existence. Although it might sound like the weakest affirmation of faith to you, it is enough to get him to respond, for as I explained yesterday, he is the ultimate reciprocator.

Do you, like that young Chinese woman I'd come to marry, feel empty? She was completely poured out due to losing so much throughout her life, including her father once and her mother twice (once to death) and another set of parents she'd come to believe were her real father and mother.

It is hard to imagine anyone emptier than she was. If you are empty, he wishes to fill you with his Spirit and with unimaginable possibilities. As she has come to know so well, he is a being more than able to keep any and all promises, and they are legion, and as far as his children are concerned, his gifts are one thing one above all—good. Good that is given to be spread to a world often bereft of and always hungering for goodness.

A QUESTION FOR YOU

If you are like me, sometimes you really enjoy the taste of a discussion served with a dash of seasoning (in the form of a question). It adds a bit of a different flavor. So take a bite and chew on this question: what punishment did those who crucified Jesus and never repent serve for committing such a reprehensible act?

According to Christian scripture and tradition, a whole nation was destroyed for this very act (the Jewish nation). If such had happened to you (think about it for a few seconds before you answer), what would you have done if you had the power to resurrect yourself, and the absolute power to enact vengeance?

This is why I am glad that I and the majority of humanity (even those purporting to serve God) are not the Almighty and are indeed very different from him. Had someone without cause put me through such, I would make sure they had what was coming.

If someone put my innocent son to death in such a horrible manner, it would be even worse, for the fires of deepest pit in hell couldn't be hot enough to fulfill my need for vengeance. 9/24/24

So, what punishment did those crucifying Jesus and who never repented suffer? No punishment whatsoever. I understand you might find my assertion incredulous, but that is one of the major problems with most religions (and Christian denominations) today. We are so quick to pass judgment in as extreme terms as possible on nonbelievers in our often misguided attempts to reach them, but we end up hurting our cause for existing in doing so. In other words, we frustrate the Originator's grand plan and our purpose. This is why understanding this question and its answer is so important to those who would truly find the path to enlightenment.

How, you may ask, is it possible such a wretched act incur no retribution? Simple. He upon whom this act was visited and he who died for the sins of the whole world (both being the same person) so he could be the perfect intercessor asked they be forgiven.

This is recorded in Luke 23:34 when he said while still hanging in agony,

[34] Forgive them, Father, for they know not what they do.

This sure doesn't sound very human, does it? As a matter of fact, it doesn't remind me of very many who call themselves Christians today either (which is a sad thing to say).

By now, you are probably wondering where I am going with this line of reasoning. As I was contemplating this thought, another scripture came to mind (which is why you should educate yourself, for knowledge that doesn't exist can't be retrieved). The scripture, Luke 12:48, records Jesus as saying, "[48] But he that knew not, and did commit things worthy of stripes, shall be beaten with few stripes. For unto whomsoever much is given, of him shall be much required: and to whom men have committed much, of him they will ask the more."

Another scripture I'd like to add in support of the point I am making is found in Mark 16:15-16:

[15] And he said unto them, Go ye into all the world, and preach the gospel to every creature.

[16] He that believeth and is baptized shall be saved; but he that believeth not shall be damned.

Also consider what the ultimate authority, for he is the Word incarnate, said concerning this matter in John 9:39-41:

[39] And Jesus said, For judgment I am come into this world, that they which see not might see; and that they which see might be made blind.

[40] And some of the Pharisees which were with him heard these words, and said unto him, Are we blind also?

[41] Jesus said unto them, If ye were blind, ye should have no sin: but now ye say, We see; therefore your sin remaineth.

In John 9:39, concerning the phrase "that they which see not might see," Jesus is speaking of those never having been exposed to the plan of salvation as it was first foretold, for those Jesus was speaking of here were the Gentiles. The Law of Moses and the many prophets sent by God pointed to Jesus and the necessity of faith in coming to know God and his will. Since the Gentiles weren't exposed to either the Law of Moses or the words of the prophets, neither did they, nor could they, see. After Christ's death and resurrection, the truth was extended to all, not just the Jews, enabling all to have sight.

Concerning the phrase "That they which see might be made blind," which is in the same verse, Jesus is speaking of the Jews, for they had been given the means whereby they should have been able to see the truth, yet most rejected it. This is why, through the prophets, God laments as he calls both Israel and Judah, his people, an adulterous whore. Because of Abraham he chose them and made a way for them, and they rejected it (the truth). After Jesus's death and resurrection, they had no excuse and were rendered blind because for the next two thousand years, they would live in exile. This was the Jewish people's punishment for rejecting what God, through Christ, had offered in the plan of salvation and reconciliation intended for not only them but all of mankind.

In John 9:40 we see the Pharisees could not accept the reality of their own state of blindness, for they were God's "chosen people." The world is now full of modern-day people analogous of the Jews, for the truth has been known and rejected throughout all Europe, the Americas and, indeed, most of the world. Many today have no excuse for their blindness, for they have been exposed to the truth.

In John 9:41 Jesus tells the Pharisees, "If ye were blind, ye should have no sin." Here, he is saying that if they had not been exposed to the truth as given through the law and the many prophets, they would not be culpable.

He goes on to say in that same verse, "But now ye say, We see; therefore your sin remaineth." Here, he condemns the Pharisees and, indeed, the entire Jewish nation. In the year AD 70, Jerusalem was destroyed by the Romans, and the Jewish people were dispersed.

The Pharisees and Jewish people, having for hundreds of years been exposed to the truth through the Law of Moses and through prophecy, were doubly guilty of rejecting the truth that comes only through faith in God's plan of salvation. The reason Jesus declared the Pharisees' (and, by extension, the Jews') sin remained is they, being exposed to the truth as revealed at the time, had already rejected it even though they were religious leaders of God's chosen people. This goes to prove being a religious leader does not mean one follows the will of God or even knows God.

The point here is those condemned to hell were done so only after rejecting the truth of Jesus's death and resurrection in atonement for humanity's sins. The main reason we are called to accept Jesus's atonement is it is God's perfect will and has been since before the foundation of the world, for such was to be for Adam. It makes us children of God and unlocks a storehouse of unlimited Holy Spirit powered possibilities made available to each and every believer so God's will can be accomplished in everyday life.

Now in life, we all make extrapolations drawing from many sources, and I have done so here by pulling two verses of scripture from the same author—Luke, a couple from Mark, and a few from John. If you are wondering what I am attempting to say, I'll make it as simple as possible: we are not punished for ignorance. We humans of all creeds are judged by what we know to be true in our limited capacity. This makes perfect sense and is the perfect combination of justice and mercy I personally believe the Originator of existence to possess.

Another piece of scripture that reinforces my point is found in Acts 10, concerning a Roman centurion named Cornelius. Now Cornelius wasn't a Jew, nor was he a Christian, yet when he prayed earnestly to God and because he did so with a right spirit and heart, God heard him and told him of Simon Peter. After meeting Peter, Cornelius and his whole household found their purpose for existence. After meeting Peter, Cornelius and his family found salvation through the cross and were, for the first time, true children of God.

I've heard sermons stating (other than the prayer for forgiveness) only true Christians have access to God's ear because Jesus is our (each individual's) only intercessor.

They use John 9:31:

[31] Now we know that God heareth not sinners: but if any man be a worshipper of God, and doeth his will, him he heareth.

In this verse, we have a man speaking of his own accord, not a declaration of Jesus, a prophet, or one of the apostles. However, what the man said was true in the sense that a sinner cannot expect to continue in sin and expect to ask for God's blessings or have a positive and growing relationship with God.

Also, remember, concerning the above verse, what Goliath said to David in 1 Samuel 17:44:

[44] And the Philistine said to David, Come to me, and I will give thy flesh unto the fowls of the air, and to the beasts of the field.

Just because something is proclaimed in the Bible, unless it is done so by one under God's authority, does not make it the truth in God's eyes.

So for those postulating God never gives ear to sinners, I ask, what about Cornelius? It is a good thing he lived near where the apostles were, for according to what many hold to be true, he would have burned in hell had the apostles not been nearby. Still, God found favor with someone having very little understanding or knowledge of the god he was so desperately and valiantly trying to serve. But how could this be if Cornelius had no intercessor or knowledge of the intercessor Cornelius so readily accepted when given the chance?

The point is, the Originator made a way for one who was willing, and this I believe he will always do. For those who never have the chance to know God, I do not know how God will reconcile them, but nowhere does it say those never rejecting the truth will be sent to hell for the reason of ignorance alone.

Addendum: Near the end of the book, there is a an in-depth discussion on this subject based on thorough research. The following had me ostracized because I wasn't willing to recant what I still hold to be true based on scripture presented. Doing otherwise would make me a hypocrite and liar, if I professed to believe differently. I do NOT believe a just, merciful God would condemn one for lack of knowledge. Jesus said the same multiple times. That is good enough for me. (end)

Now replace Cornelius's name with Sieda, a young Muslim girl never really given the chance to know of or understand the Good News (Gospel) of our purpose for being, much less practice it. She begins each day with earnest, heartfelt prayer to the one god she believes in.

She is kindhearted and would hurt no one. Before the day is over, she will pray two more times before going to bed. She knows when she prays, her heart is lifted up, and she is motivated to do even more good in her god's name and for his pleasure. She is chaste and, except for her religion, would be a daughter any Christian would love to have.

At fifteen, she dies, never having been exposed to the intercessor in any manner other than being told he is a prophet who was a good man, but to believe he is God is apostasy. Further extrapolating and bringing the previous three points into convergence, you make your own decision, but keep in mind what Jesus says about judging others so harshly: "Judge not—for as ye judge others, you shall be judged" (Matthew 7:1-2).

Why does scripture state this last phrase? It is quite simple on more than one point:

1. How dare we, so limited in knowledge and understanding, so readily condemn others?
2. When we try to reach others through condemnation, we only drive them away, and that certainly isn't in the Originator's mind.

For this reason, the two groups Jesus condemned the most were the Sadducees and Pharisees, two religious or political groups during Jesus's lifetime. One group (does this not sound familiar in today's world?) was very liberal in their scriptural interpretations, while the other was extremely conservative, yet both missed the point of their (or our) existence. Usually, those on the extreme side of any issue will be one thing above all—extremely wrong.

Another point I'd like to make should be heeded by many who in no way see their error, the conservatives. This a say as one who hold many conservative views. I feel for conservatives, for many erringly believe themselves to be doing God's will just as did the Pharisees. Yet it was the Pharisees who condemned and crucified Jesus and with good reason, for Jesus condemned them above all others.

The Pharisees were the ones most self-righteous, and in my belief and according to scripture, none of us are righteous in and of our own selves. Now I hold many conservative tenets—love of family, patriotism—when it is focused in the right direction, a strong sense of self-reliance based on a belief in and derived from (I believe) a power greater than myself. Being conservative or liberal isn't wrong, but how you deal with others from either position can be very wrong in the eyes of the Originator.

If you are wondering, well then, how do I reach others and show them their purpose for existing? Simple. Love them, and do unto them as you would have them do unto you. That too is scriptural, and it draws them to the Originator rather than push them (to or away). Leading someone is so much easier than pushing them. That I learned as a child growing up on a farm when I had to herd or coax animals. Experience is a great teacher.

TO DO GOOD BY FIGHTING EVIL OR TO FIGHT EVIL BY DOING GOOD?

Since Lucifer's rebellion and his subsequent change in nature and name (now Satan), a battle has raged, which we as humans can only begin to imagine. Every observable ill in the world around us is but a physical manifestation of a war that, if we could see it, would stagger our sense of reality.

The stakes in this war, a war that has already been decided, are tremendous, for the state in which we each will spend all eternity is decided in this realm of existence. It is decided by the choices we make and the actions we take as we respond to the circumstances we find ourselves in each and every day on a daily basis.

All in all, what is going to happen is pretty much preordained, for the will of God cannot be countermanded. But your place in what is unfolding as it happens isn't preordained. Your place in the grand scheme of things is pretty much up to you and is decided by how you respond to either what God has to offer or what Satan has to offer.

It is pretty much accepted by Christian theologians that those who choose to wrap themselves in the flesh, its trappings, and what it has to offer to the exclusion of the call by God to repent and come into his family are bound for perdition, whereas those who repent and are saved are bound for eternal glory in an existence we can't even begin to dream of.

But here, I wish to discuss only those who call themselves Christians, for they too will have a great deal to answer for according to their works here on earth. In the next realm, there will be a vast difference in the levels of power and authority each member of God's family will hold.

Some who think they are doing God's work and who believe they will be greatly rewarded shall be terribly disappointed when their station in heaven is revealed. Others, whom many think will be on the bottom rung in the afterlife, will hold positions of great significance.

How, you may ask, have I arrived at this conclusion? I have done so by reading, for such is clearly revealed in the scripture.

In this great war raging, those who decided to join forces with God by accepting Jesus's sacrifice become a Spirit-filled, triune being. Once this happens, a change takes place, and a force or power is available to each and every Christian.

This power is far beyond our comprehension and is to be used, but we see so little use of it in today's church or churches. Without a doubt, this causes God great anguish, for he wishes his children to live dynamic and productive spiritual lives.

Such enables spiritual growth far beyond what we see in most Christians today. Such also enables God to reveal himself through those willing to act in accordance to God's never-changing will. Those acting in accordance with the will of God are able to do so only because they have a great deal of faith in God's goodness and benevolence. Such faith pleases God, for such children are fearless and selfless in how they treat others, both the saved and the unsaved, both friends and enemies. This is why Jesus could tell us to love our enemies.

There are two ways most believers attempt to please God. Many try to please God in doing good by fighting evil. This we shall discuss first, for the Pharisees during Jesus's time fell into this category, as do many of the preachers in many of today's denominations. And while some of the prophets of the Old Testament seemed called to do just this, this is also a dangerous course to take in anyone's journey to heaven. It is wrought with many pitfalls that have swallowed well-meaning people and kept them from maturing as they should have; therefore, their lives show little spiritual fruit, if any.

This type of Christians and denominations, which harp on evil and rail against its sundry manifestations through various sins, often fall prey to certain pitfalls and have done so repetitively throughout history. Even before Christianity, this same problem was seen in the two prominent Jewish religions of that time, the Sadducees and the Pharisees.

When Jesus came along, his chief rival and those responsible for his crucifixion, the Pharisees, fell into this category. They saw sin in almost everything and, because of this, condemned many things God really didn't care about. By doing this, they piled so many unnecessary rules on the Jewish people that they could hardly bear the burden and often stumbled because of the stringent rules set forth by the Pharisees.

By setting rules having nothing to do with the heart or faith, the Pharisees were able to, by observing such rules themselves, set themselves above others, if only in their own minds. Yet they forgot mercy and charity, or if they showed charity, it was just that—all for show, as was much of what they did.

Jesus condemned them for such, going so far as to say they swallowed a camel while straining at a gnat. The Pharisees had set up so many rules having little to do with God's law, for their keeping such rules gave the appearance of godliness, but they forgot or overlooked God's true nature, which is goodness, benevolence, mercy, and forgiveness as well as justice. The naked truth is, they weren't as worried about pleasing and honoring God as they were about pleasing and honoring themselves by adhering to their own self-righteous standards. Such often gave them positions of power or prominence in the eyes of others.

Many who try to do good by fighting evil would be the first to hurl a stone at the woman the Pharisees brought before Jesus after she was caught committing adultery. She would have died and gone to hell had not a merciful savior intervened and forgave her after everyone had slinked away, for there was no one innocent that day but he who could forgive sin. And that day, he chose not to condemn her, but rather to extend the yet nail-scarred hand of mercy and forgiveness. Oh, that we were more Christlike.

I am not saying there should be no standards, but the standards should be mainly for the good of society and for those within the Body of Christ. Those outside the Body of Christ are only following their nature, and condemning them is unnecessary, for until they come to Christ, they are already condemned. Their hearing more condemnation being heaped on them will only drive them away, and it diminishes the Christian's ability to serve God in a charitable Christlike manner.

What is a charitable Christlike manner? It is a manner in which the Spirit of God is manifested as it was in Jesus's life—through the evidence of signs and miracles. Jesus said signs and miracles would follow all true believers. Signs and miracles testify of God, his power, and his goodness—for goodness, as seen in Jesus's life, follows true believers in accordance to God's will. As a Christian grows in spirit, the signs and miracles should increase, not decrease, as needed.

Jesus's ministry wasn't mainly railing against sin and sinners (except the Pharisees and Sadducees). His main ministry was healing the sick, raising the dead, freeing the possessed, forgiving and liberating those bound by sin, and teaching his followers and whoever would listen how to come to God. Jesus did not nearly so much do good by fighting evil as he fought evil by doing good.

If you focus on evil, evil becomes your focus. If you focus on good, good sets you free to do God's will with ever-increasing abundance. As God blesses you, you are more able to share his goodness with others, believers and nonbelievers. This both edifies the church and brings the unsaved to the altar of salvation. This, in a nutshell, fulfills God's purpose for each of us.

If you study scripture and pray fervently, you will get to know God intimately. If you really get to know God, you will see he is, above all, good. If you come to realize his goodness, you will trust him, and he will not fail you—ever.

If you come to realize he never fails you, your faith increases daily as he proves himself daily, one day at a time, by enabling you to share, not hoard, his blessings. As you share his blessings, again, the Church is edified, and God's family increases in faith and number, and God is pleased. His ability to pour his blessings into and through you is as infinite as he is: you are the only thing limiting what he is capable of doing in and through you.

Faith—it is fettered by only one thing, the thing that brought Lucifer down: self-will. Do you, as a triune child of God, wish to see signs and miracles manifested in your life? Are you willing to step out and show the world what it so wishes to see? Are you willing to reveal the power of God to the world by becoming selfless and, in doing so, unleash the true potential of unfettered faith?

ADDENDUM TO THE GIFT OF PROPHECY

I would like to delve a bit deeper into the gift of prophecy as I personally have experienced it in my own life. The gift of prophecy is the one gift Paul admonished Christians to covet, for it edifies the Body of Christ. I would like to emphasize I will never call myself a prophet as some do, for that is a great presumption I am not willing to make, and such a claim tends to be puffed up with pride.

The gift of prophecy, like any gift of the Spirit, isn't under the control of the possessor. It is, as should be the possessor, under the control of God alone. Unfortunately, the possessor, unlike the gift, can stray from God's control and does so from time to time, for he or she is all too human and even the greatest prophets have come short of complete compliance with God's will. Moses himself fell short, and because of this, he wasn't allowed to enter the Promised Land.

In even the greatest prophets' lives, the actual revelation of prophecy seemed to be a rare occurrence. The minor prophets seemed to have very few, but often important messages given to them.

In my own personal life, I can look back and see through the years a few times when God, for some reason, made the future known to me. Sometimes, I knew it was some type of prophecy just after such occurred. Other times I had no idea until what had been revealed actually happened (much to my surprise sometimes).

Never, though, could I peer into the future at will, for as I mentioned earlier, all gifts are under the control of only God.

Some of what I recount here will be a bit redundant, for I mentioned some of it earlier in this book of blogs as I was blogging. Still, I feel led to list some of what I can recall concerning the times I have, for some reason, been able to see what is to come before it happens. I had a pastor tell me yesterday that he believed I might just have a good sense of intuition. While some things can be attributed to intuition, others simply can't.

One thing I do not understand and is a bit perplexing is not all things make sense as far as my having seen them before they actually came to pass. Still, they happened, and I shall recount them in the following.

The first event occurred when I was in the first grade. One night, I dreamed I found a black plastic spider about the size of a child's hand. I found it buried in some leaves underneath a bush.

A few days later, my mother returned from Savannah (we lived on a farm thirty miles from Savannah) with a hard black plastic spider with a pencil sharpener inside of it. I was a bit amazed, for it looked exactly like the spider in the dream.

The next day, or maybe a couple of days later, I took it to school and placed it in my desk. When it came time for recess I left it in my desk when I went outside (I am sure of this). When I came back in from recess, I looked in my desk to retrieve it, and it was nowhere to be found.

As I rifled through my desk, looking for it, my teacher Ms. Knight asked, "What are you doing, Sammy?"

I remembered the dream and knew of an azalea bush near the front of the school like the one in my dream and asked if I could go out and get my sharpener, for I knew where it was. Back then, the world was much safer, and she let me go out for a moment.

I went out, looked under the azalea bush, and began digging through the leaves piled around the base of the plant to protect the roots. As I dug around in the leaves, it was as if I was reliving the dream. I quickly found the big black spider just as I had in my dream a few nights before. That was over forty-six years ago.

The next occurrence of such a dream was when I was seventeen. I used to pray every night, which I began doing in the fourth grade. One night, I dreamed God was trying to explain the Holy Spirit's relationship to the Father and the Son. In it, he tried to tell me it was analogous to the blood relationship between my father and I and, even further, the rest of our family. I know this seemed like a grandiose dream, but it seemed so real, and though I didn't understand it at all, I always felt it was from God.

Then thirty-five years later, while living in Amsterdam, I came upon a piece of scripture contained in a long-lost book found in Nag Hammadi, Egypt. When I read it, it revealed what I had always wondered since having that dream. Somehow, God had revealed thirty-five years earlier a truth I would travel thousands of miles to learn. God is indeed mysterious.

When I was in my early twenties, I attended a very strict charismatic-type church. Shortly after going there, things began happening that amazed me. One thing that happened is, I had a dream where it was as if I was hovering far above the Earth. I saw clouds hanging over the oceans and landmasses, as the Earth spun slowly. I then heard a voice telling me I was one of a certain number who were chosen. It didn't, however, tell me what purpose I was chosen for. I now believe the writing of this book was the purpose God had called me to, and my going to Amsterdam was for that purpose.

When I was in my mid-twenties, I decided to fast and pray for a full week, for I desired a greater burden for lost souls. Having only a few years earlier been diagnosed as a diabetic, I didn't really understand the dangers in doing such.

I ended up in a coma for four days and, I believe, literally spent some time in hell. The horrors are indescribable. Yet on the last day (or few hours) of the coma, things changed. Then I saw things I didn't understand. Now, with the advent of the computer, I understand them much more clearly, for it has made such happenings much more visible and acceptable in the world today.

When I awoke from the coma, I was terrified, so I called my pastor. I recounted what had happened, and he said he believed I'd seen hell. I then asked him to pray for me, which he did. That night, I dreamed I was in the most beautiful place I'd ever seen. Then I heard a voice telling me, "Whenever you have a need, you will receive whatever you need, as you need it."

Two hours after I awoke the next morning, I received a phone call from the hospital billing office. The lady asked if I had insurance or the means to pay. I was unemployed and had no insurance. When she told me the cost for four days in the hospital was $5,000, I couldn't believe it. I also couldn't believe she was hitting me with such being as I'd just came out of a coma. I was angry when I slammed the phone down on the receiver.

Two hours later, I received another phone call from the billing office. Recognizing her voice, I instantly became agitated. But when she informed me I need not worry about the bill for someone had taken care of it, I immediately remembered the voice from the night before telling me, "Whenever you have a need, you will receive whatever you need as you need it." Such has happened in my life ever since that night, and those who really know me well will attest to this truth, for God has taken care of every need as it came up.

When married to my ex-wife, I used to pray God would bless and keep our marriage together, for I believed marriage was always for life, even if the partner up and left the believer. My ex-wife hated anything to do with religion, and the closer I drew to God, the more contentious she, an already contentious person, became.

I used to walk a road in front of our house and pray every night. One night, as I prayed, a thought concerning scripture popped into my head. The thought "Two oxen unevenly yoked" deals with 2 Corinthians 6:14 and speaks of the difficulty of serving God when the partner is unsaved and against it. Still, I believed marriage was forever and had prayed God bless ours, so I put the thought out of my mind and continued walking and praying.

Again, the thought popped into my mind, but this time more forcibly. This time, I asked God if it was his will for my wife and me to separate. If it was, I was willing to acquiesce, thinking I would go on to preach in this strict denomination, which still followed most of the Jewish Law not pertaining to the rituals of sacrifice.

Within two or three months, my ex-wife filed for divorce. I, at one time, condemned divorcees who'd remarried to their face. Now God was showing me how wrong I'd been. When I went to the empty bedroom where my four- and six-year-old sons had played only nights before, the pain was unbearable. Gone was the conviction I could, or ever would, preach in this denomination again, although many of the elders and some of the ministers had confirmed my calling.

Still, there was this belief I could never remarry and would have to spend my life condemned to abject loneliness. Desperate, I began to search the scriptures.

During this time (about a year and one-half after the divorce), I found 1 Corinthians 7:15:

[15] But if the unbelieving depart, let him depart. A brother or a sister is not under bondage in such cases: but God hath called us to peace.

Although this verse was unambiguous, I had a hard time releasing a belief I once held so firmly, so I began to pray over the matter. One night soon thereafter, I had a dream where I saw my ex-wife holding a little baby girl (we'd had two boys). Her boyfriend was there also, but there was a barbed-wire fence between them, and she was desperately trying to pull him through it but couldn't. When I awoke, I immediately knew the meaning of the dream.

Later that very day, I called her. She was aware of my ability to sometimes see into the future. Just after we began to talk, I told her she would be having a daughter, and she and her boyfriend would never get along.

She began to curse before asking who told me, for she told me she had learned only the day before that she was pregnant. Even then, she was unaware of the sex of the fetus. Six months later, she gave birth to a little girl, and she and her boyfriend, though still together, have never lived in harmony. (Addendum: they divorced)

I then began praying for a Christian wife but fell in love with a girl from Beijing, China, who was an atheist. She later converted, and we ended up eloping. I told her God would take care of us, and though we were both unemployed and her father withdrew his financial support, we both graduated from the University of Georgia through grants and a program I was under called Vocational Rehabilitation (to help me due to diabetes).

Shortly after graduating, we settled on the farm my parents owned, and I cleared the land and planted numerous fruit trees. One day, I felt we would soon move and she would have a new job, so I informed her of such. I didn't know where, but I knew it would be soon, and I even told her what her pay would be. In four months, we moved from near Savannah to New Orleans, and she made what I had said she would.

The week before Katrina, I told her we'd again be moving soon and there was no need to worry for God would take care of us. Why I said this, I didn't know, but I knew it would come to pass. The Friday before Katrina hit, there was a convention given by the Promise Keepers being held in Mobile, Alabama. A few of the men from the church I was attending at the time and I went to it and were to spend Friday night, all of Saturday, and Sunday listening to Christian music and enjoying sermons and fellowship.

That Saturday morning, I turned the radio on and learned Katrina was strengthening and had turned. It had now drawn a bead on New Orleans, so I hopped in my SUV and headed home.

Two weeks later, we were living in a very nice town house in an upscale neighborhood called the Woodlands, which is near Houston, Texas. Her company first provided the town house in Texas and then a full-size mobile home on our property near New Orleans until we moved into our new home almost four years later. Again, all went as I was led to foretell.

When we began building our post-Katrina house, I told her God would provide as he always had for us. Months, and then over a years passed, and my government FEMA grant was being slow walked. I did not understand why until after the two thousand and seven housing crash, which enabled me to build my home at significant savings because prices dropped significantly on almost everything. We were able to build a house I somehow feel I do not deserve but am thankful for. God is great.

As the completion of this book neared, I felt, as strongly as ever, led to proclaim we would be moving from Amsterdam back to New Orleans. I felt so strongly this time; and since it tied into what I was writing of in the blogs that came to be this book, I wrote in a June 17 blog on MySpace that my wife, our son, and I would be moving back within three months, and that God would see all went well. You can still see it there in my June 18 MySpace blog.

My wife had no new job offers, and her old job wasn't willing to transfer her back. The situation at her company of thirteen years also did something she found untenable, something they'd done before, so she came to talk to her boss (a new hire), but he wouldn't give her the time of day. The next day, she went to a new job interview and, a couple of days later, after being told she'd hear back in a week, was hired.

Within three weeks, I was back, and God had done quite a few miraculous things necessary to make sure we were taken care of so this book could be printed.

I could recount a few more incidents concerning prophecy as it relates to my life, but I think you get my point.

The word *edify* means "to educate morally or spiritually or to instruct in spiritual matters." The writing of this book and of the ensuing prophecy concerning God's providence in our moving back to see its publication coming to fruition serves that purpose.

When you selflessly step out in boldness to accomplish God's will, the impossible is easily attainable, for it is not of or about self, and the miracles and signs accompanying God's provision in carrying out his will are excellent testimonies to both believers and unbelievers alike. It is about trust – in God.

Believers are encouraged to step out in faith, which enables them to do more in the service of God. Nonbelievers marvel in that they are able to see there is, indeed, more to life than what the five senses are able to register. In both cases, more nonbelievers are drawn to make the commitment that enlarges the Body of Christ and increases the number of triune beings now making up the family of God, the original triune being.

In this, the material realm, only that which has substance or the ability be measured can be experienced. Faith, however, draws from another plane of existence, for read what the Bible says concerning faith in Hebrews 11:1:

[1] Now faith is the substance of things hoped for, the evidence of things not seen.

Faith, alone, is able to reach into the spiritual realm of God and bring into being what we can only touch by faith. But faith is capable of doing so only to the extent that faith is unfettered.

Because I am in a great deal of pain today, this took a bit longer than anticipated. Hopefully it is written in a cogent manner. Please pray for me, as this has been going on for the past few days and is really wearing on me. Thanks!

ADDENDUM: WHAT CAUSED ADAM AND EVE TO FALL FROM GRACE

It seems Adam and Eve had it everything going for them. In all of creation they, alone, were made in God's image. Everything should have been perfect. They lived in a Garden where their every need was taken care of. I can imagine them walking through the Garden on a cool morning with the dew drenched grass wetting their toes as they talked to God, who was there in person.

It was like a cloudless sky, perfection personified, but storm clouds were forming on the horizon, for there was one being in creation that wasn't happy at all. The serpent lurked - waiting for an opportunity.

Have you ever wondered why Satan hated humanity or how a speaking serpent could have beguiled Eve? I don't know about you, but a talking serpent would have caused me to jet away as fast as my two bare feet could have moved me.

As to why Satan showed an incredible amount of animosity to Adam and Eve, I've done a great deal of research and I am quite sure I have it figured out. Am I 100 % sure? I'm not. But I have found no other reason that comes anywhere near to what I am about to propose.

Lucifer held a higher station than any other angel in all of heaven. He was also the most beautiful being ever created. Imagine when he realized God's plan for Adam and Eve. Imagine how he felt when he realized the gift God gave them, which caused them, unlike any other creature, to be made "in God's image".

Suddenly Satan's status as the epitome of perfection, concerning creation, was eclipsed. And the creatures that had displaced him were made of nothing but soil. Yet this sack of soil contained a portion of God, himself; something no angel possessed.

I have read from a non-canonical gospel (I put little faith in such), the Gospel of Thomas, in which Satan says Adam and Eve's creation caused him to fall from grace. Satan also claims in this apocryphal gospel that this was why he beguiled Eve.

Verses found in both Isaiah and Ezekiel say pride caused his fall. It's easy to imagine Satan's feelings and pride being hurt when suddenly a creature, not too unlike all other flesh and blood creatures (when compared to spiritual beings), was given a blessing no other in creation had ever been blessed with. Because of this gift these new creatures, made of soil, became true children of God, for they physically possessed the Holy Ghost.

Satan (because he can be in only one place at a time) wasn't always in God's physical presence. Adam and Eve's sack of flesh carried God wherever they went, so they were always in God's immediate, physical presence. Satan couldn't stomach this reality; therefore, he rebelled against God and God's plan for humanity. After his fall Satan formed a plan to undo what God had done. I used the term physical presence because God's spirit is everywhere (omnipresent).

The most effective way to do this also would be punish the two he held responsible, Adam and Eve. Satan means accuser, for he'd rather do that than accept responsibility for his actions. Also, since he couldn't directly punish God, he could do so very effectively by corrupting God's only children at that time, Adam, and Eve.

So, Satan had a plan. The only thing he needed was opportunity. Genesis 3 begins by saying the serpent was subtler than any other beast that God had created. We all know that the serpent was really Satan. But how could he, in the form of a serpent, beguile Eve?

Why he would appear as a talking serpent had always perplexed me. I've always thought it was merely a metaphor. But exhaustive research has led me to another conclusion, for a talking serpent doesn't seem very crafty; it seems strange. Also, it didn't seem such would be capable of enticing someone who'd walked with God, and who'd done so as his child. Furthermore, when you consider the penalty for disobedience was spiritual suicide, an ordinary talking serpent didn't seem to be a good candidate for such a monumental task.

In Genesis 3 Satan is said to appear before Eve in the form of a talking Serpent. Desiring to dig a bit deeper into the matter, I Googled the Ancient Hebrew equivalents of the word *serpent* s used in scripture to better understand the various English translations of the word "serpent". What I found was amazing. What's more amazing is that, when cross-referenced, more than one verse supports my conclusion. I don't put much faith in any biblical argument not supported by cross-referencing and the more supporting verses the better.

The Hebrew word for serpent is nachash. Nachash can function as a noun, a verb, or an adjective. As a noun is means a snake or a serpent. As a verb it means to practice divination, enchantments, or interpret omens. When used as an adjective "nachash" means "shining". The Hebrew word used in Genesis 3 was the adjective form of "nachash", for it had "ha" (meaning the) before it. Ha-nachash, therefore, means "the shining one" in Genesis 3.

Therefore, Satan didn't appear to Eve as your everyday talking serpent. Rather, he appeared as a beautiful shining being whose very appearance would have influenced Eve's attitude towards him in a positive manner. Far from being repulsed by a serpent, she was most likely fascinated by and enamored with this brilliant creature.

That Satan would, or even could, appear in this form in the

Garden is supported by other verses of scripture. One is Isaiah 14:12: How art thou fallen from heaven, O Lucifer, son of the morning! how art thou cut down to the ground, which didst weaken the nations! The word Lucifer is Latin in origin. According to Strong's Concordance it means "shining one" or "morning star".

Other scripture supporting my proposal is Ezekiel 28:13&14:

13) Thou hast been in Eden the garden of God; every precious stone was thy covering, the sardius, topaz, and the diamond, the beryl, the onyx, and the jasper, the sapphire, the emerald, and the carbuncle, and gold: the workmanship of thy tabrets and of thy pipes was prepared in thee in the day that thou wast created.

14) Thou art the anointed cherub that covereth; and I have set thee so: thou wast upon the holy mountain of God; thou hast walked up and down in the midst of the stones of fire.

I can imagine how Lucifer must have shined decked out in precious and semiprecious jewels. The two preceding verses show this is how he appeared in the Garden, for one mentions Eden.

Jesus also speaks of Satan and his luminous appearance when he tells his disciples in Luke 10:18: "I saw Satan fall like lightning from heaven."

Paul also makes clear that Satan is able to transform his appearance when it suites him. He gives this warning in 2nd Corinthians 11:14: And no marvel; for Satan himself is transformed into an angel of light.

All of this makes the likelihood of Satan's appearing as a beautiful, shining creature even more plausible. Yet his appearance alone couldn't possibly sway Eve in and of itself. No, he had to offer something that appeared extremely desirable – desirable enough to risk suffering the penalty of death should she do it.

So, what exactly could he offer her that would, in her mind, trump what God, as her Father, had already given her all she could ever want? Again, we must consider a certain Hebrew word.

Thatword is found in Genesis 3:5. That word is Elohim, or Elohim depending who it is speaking of.

Elohim is a word that the Hebrew language borrowed from the Canaanites. Since the Canaanites believed in many Gods, by default, elohim was plural. But when, in Hebrew, it is used with a singular verb or adjective, it is singular as in "God" (with a capital G).

Let's look at Genesis 3:5 and see what it says. This is the KJV translation, which I use when posting, because it's in public domain. Genesis 3:5: For God doth know that in the day ye eat thereof, then your eyes shall be opened, and ye shall be as gods, knowing good and evil.

As seen in this verse elohim is used twice. One, the first Elhim, is singular, which makes it "God", with a capitol "G". The second elohim, however, is plural and this makes it (the) "gods" with a small "g". Some of the more contemporary translations, however, capitalize the "G" in the second case, though exhaustive research has led me to conclude this is incorrect. It isn't that scripture is wrong, but when different versions don't agree, the translation of one of the two being compared is wrong. Older versions (including the Catholic text) use a small case "g". Using either upper case "G" or lower case "g" makes all the difference in the world.

Reading it the way it is presented in the King James Version makes clear just what Satan offered her. After lying and assuring her she would not die, he assured her that if she switched allegiance by believing him, rather than God, he would give her knowledge hat would make her like unto him. She, he told her, would become this radiant being forbidden. Such he has used throughout history.

Eve believed the lie and, in doing so, she disbelieved God. That, in and of itself, was the original sin, for in doing this she switched her allegiance. Trust is an integral ingredient in any loving relationship. When Adam followed suit, they, by believing Satan, broke the trust they'd had in their relationship with God, for in believing such, they had to also believe God was a liar.

Sin is anathema to God, thus their separation from God resulted in immediate spiritual death when the Holy Spirit immediately left their bodies. Light and dark cannot occupy the same space. But the moment trust was buried, hope sprouted, for God's will is incontrovertible.

The next question I asked myself was what sin did Adam and Eve commit when eating the apple. As I said earlier, when Eve ate the metaphorical apple, she suffered immediate spiritual death. Adam followed suit.

The forbidden fruit was, for Adam and Eve, a metaphor for disobeying God by doing a certain act God disproved of. This act of disobedience was the same as the breaking of certain commandments found in the Ten Commandments, which were given thousands of years after the lives of Adam and Eve. It was also the same as breaking one of the Two Commandments given by Jesus, as seen in Matthew 22:37-40: 37Jesus replied:

39. Love the LORD your God with all your heart and with all your soul and with all your mind.

38. This is the first and greatest commandment.

39. And the second is like it; Love your neighbor as yourself.

40. All the Law and the Prophets hang on these two commandments.

The reason the first of Jesus' two commandments is the greatest commandment is because unless it is followed, none of the rest can be truly followed. It also correlates with the Ten Commandments that deal solely with our relationship with God, who is our spiritual bedrock.

Some may say, "I'd never murder anyone!" However, if one isn't in love with God, he or she, by example, hinders, or outright stops others from accepting the gift of salvation. Spiritual murder, in a true sense, is more egregious than physical murder.

The first of the two great commandments had to do with both love and trust concerning God; two traits unable exist apart from one another. It is also analogous to the first four of the Ten Commandments in that they deal with man's relationship with God.

The Ten Commandments where first written as laws given to the Hebrew nation, although some have followed these laws through history, yet could claim no kinship to Abraham. Such men have always existed; from Melchizedek, to the three wise men who visited Jesus upon his birth. There have always been those who somehow knew and loved God without their lineage having anything to do with the lineage of Adam, a lineage recorded meticulously in the both the Old Testament and in the New Testament.

Many lived while Abraham's offspring still formed a nation (three wise men). We of the new, living covenant, who, by obeying the two commandments given by Christ, are a further example.

The first great commandment concerns love and trust in relation to God, while the second great commandment concerns the love and trust between fellow humans, without which any society unravels. The second great commandment is analogous with commandments five through ten.

Therefore, most (six) of the Ten Commandments didn't apply to either Adam or Eve, for these commandments deal with how individuals interact with other members of society. They had no reason to lie to each other, steal from each other, couldn't commit adultery, couldn't covet, or break any of the other commandments wherein one interacts with other members of society. There simply were no other humans, but them, in the Garden of Eden.

Christ, in giving his two great commandments, simply combined the Ten Commandments dealing with societal interactions (the last six) into the one found above in Matthew 22:39. If this commandment was followed, it insured that no one would act to harm his or her neighbor. Such happens when actions are motivated out of love.

We must ask again, then, what commandment(s) did Adam and Eve break? This is central as to why they fell from grace.

Again, they broke the most important of the Ten Commandments, the first. This is the most important of all commandments for this reason: if one breaks this commandment, to whom do they answer if any one of the other laws are broken? If they've already discarded God's rule over them, why take heed of the other laws? Such leads to the 'do what you want to get what you want' mentality so prevalent today.

Another reason, which is even more important, is found in Hebrews 11:6: "without faith it is impossible to please God, because anyone who comes to him must believe he exists." Not serving God is proclaiming he does not exist, for who in their right mind wouldn't want to serve a God as wonderful and as merciful as is I AM. What is tragic about Adam and Eve's sin is they, without doubt, knew God existed.

In disobeying God in the Garden of Eden, they broke the first of Jesus' two commandments. This commandment is found in Matthew 22:37: "Jesus said unto him, Thou shalt love the Lord thy God with all thy heart, and with all thy soul, and with all thy mind."

Jesus puts an emphasis on this commandment's importance when he says in Matthew 22:28: "This is the first and great commandment."

Again, the first four of the Ten Commandments and the first of the two given in the great commandments by Jesus are the same. They deal with knowing, loving, and obeying our creator, God.

Despite their intimate relationship with God (their being his beloved children), Adam and Eve broke the most important of all commandments. In doing so they switched their allegiance to Satan by believing what he said, rather than what God had said, and by wanting to be like him (like the gods), instead of being like their Creator in whose image they were made.

Their doing this led to the occurrence that always follows the breaking of the first commandment. It led to the breaking of the second commandment, which basically says you shall not make other idols.

Humans are born with a great vacuum or void inside them. This void exists for but one reason – to be filled by God's Holy Spirit. Rest assured that if God isn't filling this vacuum, something(s) else is going to fill it.

When God's Holy Spirit fills that void, one is led to worship God, for the Holy Spirit leads those who are born again of the Spirit to do just that. We worship God not only with our entire being that the Holy Spirit can empower us.

If God's Holy Spirit isn't filling this void, then that which is more than happy to fill the vacuum becomes an archetypical false god. But only the true, living God is able fill that void completely, for nothing created comes close to being as boundlessly filling as is our Creator, for He fills the entirety of creation.

There being so many vessels (people) filled with the desires of their father, Satan (we are al born thus), rather than being filled by God's Spirit, and led by His desires, is why there's so much misery in the world today, for unless God fills the void we are all born with one is compelled to continue searching for something, anything, to do what God, alone, can do. Only God can fill that void, for the void was made for but one reason – to be God's temple (1st Corinthians 6:19).

Unless one invites God to fill that void they will continue to search and, along the way, continue to suffer the gnawing pangs of discontent.

Therefore, Jesus referred to it as the first and great commandment. It is also why he posed this question: "What does it profit a man to gain the whole world, and forfeit his soul (Matthew 16:26)?"

Another subject matter I like to discuss is pure speculation, but the conclusion I've arrived at makes perfect sense, in no way contradicts God's word, and answers things many Christians may have wondered. I address how and why God was able to create Christ without Original Sin passing down to him, as it did to all other humans at birth.

God, even as he works miracles, works with what is available; even when such seems unnecessary. To defeat Satan, he used the Adamic blood line without wavering. Of course we are all of this bloodline, but God, using those few who were faithful during and after the antediluvian period, worked with what was naturally available. To emphasize this, when a prophet or judge worked a great miracle, he'd have them use a physical object when doing so.

Moses used a staff when parting the Red Sea. Elijah used his cloak to part a river. Elisha had Naman wash in the Jordan to cure his leprosy. Jesus put mud made from dirt and spit on a man's eyelids to cure his blindness. These are but a few examples proving God uses the natural when working His miracles.

So, how did God ensure original sin passed down through the generations, as it became the bane we are all born with (inherited)? While reading scripture, I asked this as I was contemplating how original sin didn't impact Jesus, as it had all ever passing through the birth canal before him. I knew it had to do with God being his father, by why and how?

Had I not taken many courses dealing with anatomy and physiology, I wouldn't have had any idea, for I had once spent two years in a small college studying to become a registered nurse. It has to do with genetics. I will keep it as simple as possible.

I propose, and this is speculation, God affixed original sin to our gender specific genes, AKA sex genes. He chose these genes because they are the only genes we possess that does not shuffle. This is the reason one can trace their paternal lineage back thousands of years if one is male by using our nuclear DNA. Women can do the same with their mitochondrial DNA (mtDNA).

All other genes shuffle, and re not assured of passing from one generation to the next. That is why a family may has children with three different eye colors, and why we can inherit the same gene our uncle has that makes one's eyes blue, although neither mom or dad had blue eyes.

By affixing original sin to the gender specific gene, God insured original sin would infect all of humanity without fail. This left the door open whereby God could not only insure jesus would not be born with original sin, but it also enabled God to become made in our likeness, just as we were made in His. This monumental event occurred when the Holy Spirit impregnated Mary, the mother of Jesus.

When the Word, Jesus (God) was born, God took on our image in the truest sense of the word. That thought boggled my mind. By bypassing the normal manner by which a child is conceived, God took a vital piece out of the equation that had insured original sin would pass to the next generation; in this case, Jesus.

As I mentioned earlier, this made Satan's crucifixion of Christ, a man who was spotless because he had no original sin, egregious enough that Jesus was able to conquer death, for death was the verdict for sin, and sin alone. Not only was Jesus born without sin, he lived a sinless life, as Paul says in Hebrews 4:15: 15 For we have not an high priest which cannot be touched with the feeling of our infirmities; but was in all points tempted like as we are, yet without sin.

The God we serve is more awesome than we can begin to fathom. To see how he was, and is able to frustrate the plans of a being more magnificent than we can imagine is beyond belief of most. But it need not be where the only thing that matters – your salvation.

As I close this book out, I hope I answered both questions you may have had for years, as well as those you've never pondered. But I have a question. Do you know, without a doubt, should you die or be killed before the day is over that God will call you home to an existence Paul describes in 1st Corinthians 2:9: But as it is written, Eye hath not seen, nor ear heard, neither have entered into the heart of man, the things which God hath prepared for them that love him.

If you are not one hundred percent sure that you are, indeed, saved, there is no time like right now to remedy what would be an eternal problem of a magnitude you cannot wrap your mind around. The extreme anguish of hell is a reality I've experience while in a four day coma.

Becoming a child of God is so easy, for Jesus did the heavy lifting over two millennia ago when he suffered a horrendous death on the cross after being beaten unmercifully. All you need to confess you are a sinner in need of salvation, for we all are or were. Then upon reflection, tell Jesus you believe he died on the cross for your sins, and that he rose from the dead of his own accord. Then repent by committing to change your life by walking away from all sinful practices, as you ask him into your heart to be your Lord and Savior.

Upon doing this, you will become as different from your former, non Spirit filled self as possible. There will be more difference between you and an unsaved person as there is an unsaved person and a rock, for both the unsaved person and the rock are spiritually dead. If you just asked Christ into your heart, I'd like to welcome you into the family, for we will have forever to get to know one another. God bless.

www.ingramcontent.com/pod-product-compliance
Lightning Source LLC
Chambersburg PA
CBHW020500030426
42337CB00011B/176